W9-BXY-842

3 1257 01031 4283

WITHDRAWN

Schaumburg Township District Library

32 West Library Lane

Schaumburg, Illinois   60194

GAYLORD

Improving Poor People

Improving Poor People

THE WELFARE STATE, THE "UNDERCLASS," AND URBAN SCHOOLS AS HISTORY

Michael B. Katz

PRINCETON UNIVERSITY PRESS

PRINCETON, NEW JERSEY

SCHAUMBURG TOWNSHIP DISTRICT LIBRARY
32 WEST LIBRARY LANE
SCHAUMBURG, ILLINOIS 60194

10/95
IN6

362.50973
KAT

3 1257 01031 4283

Copyright © 1995 by Princeton University Press
Published by Princeton University Press, 41 William Street,
Princeton, New Jersey 08540
In the United Kingdom: Princeton University Press, Chichester,
West Sussex

All Rights Reserved

Library of Congress Cataloging-in-Publication Data

Katz, Michael B., 1939–
Improving poor people : the welfare state, the "underclass,"
and urban schools as history / Michael B. Katz.
p.   cm.
Includes bibliographical references and index.
ISBN 0-691-02994-6 (alk. paper)
1. Public welfare—United States—History.
2. Urban poor—United States—History. 3. Urban schools—
United States—History. 4. Social history. 5. Social policy. I. Title.
HV91.K348   1995
362.5'0973—dc20   94-31111

This book has been composed in Palatino

Princeton University Press books are printed on
acid-free paper and meet the guidelines for permanence
and durability of the Committee on Production
Guidelines for Book Longevity of the
Council on Library Resources

Printed in the United States of America

1 2 3 4 5 6 7 8 9 10

For my graduate students,
PAST AND PRESENT

Contents

Acknowledgments

THIS BOOK draws on almost thirty years of work. In that time I have acquired many intellectual and personal debts. Here, I will acknowledge only some of the proximate ones immediately relevant to this book.

Chapter 1 draws on my earlier work on the history of welfare. A somewhat different version was written for a series of conferences on comparative welfare history held at the Werner Reimers Stiftung in Bad Homburg, Germany, which provided generous support, and will be published in a book that I have coedited with Christoph Sachsse, *The Mixed Economy of Welfare: Private/Public Relations in England, Germany, and the United States from the 1870s to the 1930s*. I want to thank both the Stiftung and the participants in the conference for their helpful comments.

An early version of chapter 2, which draws on my work on the intellectual history of responses to poverty, was written for the centennial of the Henry Street Settlement in New York. I appreciate the honor conferred by the invitation to lecture at the centennial celebration of an institution with such a rich legacy. My work on poverty was immeasurably enriched by my participation as project archivist in the work of the Social Science Research Council's Committee for Research on the Urban Underclass, and I especially want to thank the committee's excellent staff—Martha Gephart, Robert Pearson, Raquel Ovryn Rivera, Alice O'Connor—for their courtesy and for the education they provided.

A portion of chapter 3 was published in *Teachers College Record* (fall 1992) as "Chicago School Reform as History" and is used with the permission of the journal. The chapter also includes adaptations of earlier essays on the origins of public education. My work on Chicago school reform has been conducted in collaboration with two marvelous and creative colleagues, Michelle Fine and Elaine Simon, and my ideas on the subject derive in large part from our work together and from conversations with them. A portion of the chapter adapts some of our article in *Catalyst*, the journal of Chicago school reform. Our work started during my year as a Visiting Fellow at the Russell Sage Foundation, which provided the time, encouragement, and stimulation to launch the project. The project has been supported generously by the Spencer Foundation. In Chicago, many people have shown us great courtesy, answering our endless questions, providing background material, giving us precious time. Entering the educational reform community there has been one of the unexpected and great joys of the project.

Chapter 4 began as a working paper for the Russell Sage Foundation. My debt to the Foundation, especially its president, Eric Wanner, is very great. A somewhat different version was published in Arnold R. Hirsch and Raymond A. Mohl, eds., *Urban Policy in Twentieth-Century America* (New Brunswick, N.J.: Rutgers University Press, 1993) and is used with the permission of the press. A grant from the Research Foundation of the University of Pennsylvania made possible the microfilming of the case records on which the discussion is based.

Three people read the introduction to this book and offered detailed, constructive advice when I was floundering with its organization and content. My gratitude toward them is great. They are Michael Frisch, Viviana Zelizer, and Mike Rose. Mike Rose's wonderful book, *Lives on the Boundary*, gave me the inspiration and courage to try to mix a bit of autobiography with more conventional writing about history. I also want to thank the two readers of this manuscript for Princeton University Press for their constructive, insightful comments. The editorial staff of Princeton University Press once again has been a joy to work with. My thanks go especially to Lauren Osborne and Beth Gianfagna. Cindy Crumrine has again proved a model copy editor.

During nearly thirty years of teaching, I have had the extraordinary fortune to work with a succession of exceptional graduate students. They have been stimulating and enjoyable intellectual companions, and I always have learned from them. Some of them have become my good friends. This book has a subtext directed to them and, I hope, their successors.

The idea for this book occurred to me in the serenity of Clioquossia in Oquossoc, Maine, where I did most of the work of revising the essays that compose it and writing the introduction. As always, I appreciate the support of friends and neighbors there as well as of my family, especially my wife, Edda, and youngest daughter, Sarah, on whom the preoccupation that accompanies writing takes the greatest toll.

Improving Poor People

Introduction

THERE ARE places where history feels irrelevant, and America's inner cities are among them. Those historians engaged with the problems of their time live, always, with an unresolved tension between activism and scholarship; they are forced on the defense by practitioners of contemporary social science and policy research, whose relentless presentism views historians as of little use other than as entertainment. Instead of advancing social reform, do historians, in fact, distract attention from children killing each other, jobless men, homeless families, failing institutions, and crumbling infrastructure? Perhaps historians who care about the future of American cities and their people should throw away their note cards, leave their libraries and archives, and work for a frontline social agency or in community economic development. Would historians committed to social reconstruction give more to the causes they champion with degrees in social work or public policy or as public interest lawyers?

Since the early 1960s, I have lived with these questions and with the tension between activism and scholarship, which I have tried to mediate with research on a number of questions about American social institutions, public policy, and reform. Why have American governments proved unable to redesign a welfare system that satisfies anyone? Why has public policy proved unable to eradicate poverty and prevent the deterioration of major cities? What strategies have helped poor people survive the poverty endemic to urban history? How did urban schools become unresponsive bureaucracies that fail to educate most of their students? Are there fresh, constructive ways to think about welfare, poverty, and public education? Do any hopeful examples exist?

Because they traced extreme poverty to drink, laziness, and other forms of bad behavior, many nineteenth-century reformers tried to use public policy and philanthropy to improve the character of poor people rather than to attack the material sources of their misery. Reformers emphasized individual regeneration through evangelical

3

religion, temperance legislation, punitive conditions for relief, family breakup, and institutionalization. Of course, as a reform strategy, improving poor people did not end with the nineteenth or early-twentieth centuries, as almost any contemporary discussion of "welfare reform" reveals. Indeed, in the 1990s, discussions of inner-city poverty invoke an "underclass," defined primarily by bad behavior, not by poverty, and deemed to be more in need of improvement than cash.

As a strategy, improving poor people consistently has awarded education a starring role. Of all options, education has shone as the preferred solution for social problems by compensating for inadequate parenting, shaping values and attitudes, molding character, and imparting useful skills. Added to its other assignments, improving poor people has given American education an extraordinary—indeed, impossible—load, which is one reason why with regularity since the third quarter of the nineteenth century critics have alleged the failure of public schools. As the history of education shows, improving poor people not only has misdiagnosed the issues; it also time and again has deflected attention from their structural origins and from the difficult and uncomfortable responses they require.

Through the history of welfare (or relief, as it used to be called), urban poverty, and public education, this book explores attempts to improve poor people during the last two centuries. It also illustrates the public uses of history. For nearly thirty years, my excursions into the world of social science and social policy often have highlighted obsolete or distorted versions of history that undermine the conclusions of research or recommendations for policy, especially ones relating to cities and their people. In response, I have tried to show how interpretations of the past grounded in analytic social history, freed of comforting myths, can reframe discussions of great public issues.

In attempts to reframe public discussion, one of the challenges for historians remains striking the balance between persistence and discontinuity. Because some ideas, preoccupations, and responses do indeed run throughout the last two centuries, historians often overemphasize precedents, parallels, and persistence. They remain uncomfortable with radical rupture, discontinuity, abrupt transformation. Nonetheless, as the history of recent decades illustrates, these, too, form important strands of history, and, in this book, I try to explore the ways they modify the weight of the past.

Attentive readers will find tensions and inconsistencies within my work and in the chapters of this book, for I have not resolved all the issues—historical or policy related—raised by these excursions into the history of social policy and reform. Although, in part, this reflects my own limitations, at points the historical evidence complicates my own inclinations (as with local democracy, discussed below), and I can't find a neat solution to the dilemmas raised by the historical accounts. Indeed, one message of history, which flies against the grain of attempts to formulate a science of society, may be the necessity of learning to live with and negotiate between conflict and contradiction. This book tries to show that the past was untidy and that we must make our way, as best we can, among the inconsistencies and contradictions bequeathed us by the processes we join together to call history.

Three of these tensions deserve special mention. One is the relation between "private" and "public." As I point out, no definition of either term will be wholly satisfactory. Not only is their meaning multilayered, it has shifted throughout American history, leaving them more social and political constructions than fixed spheres. However defined, their relations with each other have remained tangled, difficult if not impossible to dissect, giving American social institutions, such as welfare and education, a permanently mixed economy. At one time or another, *public* and *private* have carried different emotional loadings. In the nineteenth century, even at times in the early twentieth, *public* was a term of honor signifying civic pride and the assumption of important social responsibilities by communities and government. More recently, *public* evokes corruption and incompetence in contrast to *private*, which stands for initiative and efficiency. In truth, neither sphere ever has matched its popular image. Nor is it possible to argue for the inherent superiority of one over the other. No fixed rules define boundaries or automatically place activities in one sphere or the other. The drive toward "privatization" has forced defenders of the public realm, as in education, to justify assumptions previously shared by nearly everyone, to reexamine arguments once made reflexively, to find better reasons than sentiment or precedent. This book offers data useful for more realistic, less ideologically driven or nostalgic approaches to the public/private issue; it does not resolve it.

Other tensions emerge from attempts to define the limits of localism. As a historian of bureaucracy, I know the stultifying impact that centralization exerted on public education. I have written of the repeated failures of top-down educational reform efforts and observed the weakness of social research on poverty that fails to incorporate a grass-roots perspective in its design. As an unreconstructed democrat, I remain committed to local democracy, excited by the potential of community economic development and the myriad activities directed toward rebuilding local communities. As a historian, I also know that local control has meant the perpetuation of segregation, the institutionalization of inequities through suburbanization, and a selfish rejection of social responsibility. I know that by themselves, the achievements of individual communities, of local democracy, remain limited; their resource base is too slim, their ability to staunch major wounds, such as capital flight, nonexistent, their capacity to transcend a politics of patronage questionable. What defines their appropriate sphere? In what circumstances is local democracy effective and equitable? Here, too, the historical record illuminates these questions with many examples but offers no clear or consistent answers.

Nor do I see a consistent pattern in the role of government. My work on the history of education has criticized government. Actions by state and local governments, I argue, created an excessively bureaucratic, remote, self-serving, intellectually inadequate, inequitable educational system. At the same time, I have praised the achievements of America's welfare state, despite its limits, as evidence of government's capacity to tackle major social problems. Government has shown it can lift people out of poverty, reduce hunger, and improve housing. Is it possible to criticize the organization and delivery of services without discrediting the potential and capacity of government? How should social scientists balance the perversities of government with an appreciation of its accomplishments? Historians can convey both sides of the story, as I have tried to do, but a clear resolution remains elusive.

I offer no concrete solutions. Historians and other social scientists who offer interpretative accounts of social issues always face a "last chapter" problem. Readers expect them to extract clear lessons from history, offer unambiguous recommendations, and foresee the future. My standard response—my role is to analyze and explain the problem; I have no special expertise in devising solutions—although honest, rarely satisfies. When historians tack on a set of conclusions, more often than not they appear utopian, banal, not very different from what others have suggested, marginally related to the analysis that precedes them and far less subtle. The reason, of course, is that no set of recommendations flows directly from any historical analysis. Understanding the origins and dimensions of a social issue can lead in very different policy directions.

How then should one conceptualize the role of the historian in policy? Where can the historian be most useful? At a recent conference of the Social Science Research Council's Committee for Research on the Urban Underclass, an official of the Department of Housing and Urban Development explained the possible points of intervention to the assembled collection of researchers, policy analysts and advocates, and program directors, who had gathered to start to think about a common research agenda. One point occurs during the formulation of the assumptions on which policy is to be built. Another happens when the concrete outlines of policy are being drawn. A third opens during the design of the implementation process. The most appropriate level for academic researchers, and in many ways the most influential, he argued, was the first, the formulation of assumptions. This is one of the ways I have hoped my own work, including this book, might play some small part. The chapters that follow contain several examples of historical interpretations that might inform the assumptions undergirding policy. One, discussed in chapter 2, is whether circumstances in today's inner cities represent a situation new in American history or an intensification of old patterns. Failure to appreciate the novelty of the current situation, I argue, has inhibited effective responses.

Clearly, though, history has meaning for women and men on the front line of social action. Nothing has pleased me more throughout nearly three decades of writing on the history of social policy than letters, telephone calls, and comments from teachers, community activists, or the staff of local programs who have read something I have written and found it important or useful. Usually, I am not sure what they find meaningful. They know the issues and institutions far better than I ever will. I offer them no concrete suggestions. One reason is the limits of my expertise; equally important is my conviction that experts telling people what to do is part of the problem, that the best solutions will emerge from conversations among the involved parties, that if I could do anything, it would be to start those conversations and help them along.

I think people on the ground sometimes find reassurance and legitimation in academic work. Academics validate their discontents, reassure them they are not crazy or paranoid, and give them ammunition for their fights. I think, too, we help them avoid blaming themselves by giving them the information to understand their situation better. They learn to locate themselves in time and space; they see the press of history and the web of connections that anchors their activities and constrains change. The converse—the danger of history—is demoralization. The weight of the past, the inertia of institutions, the power of special interests loom so great that action appears futile. Why even try? Here, I think, is where the special responsibility of the historian lies. It is to rebut presumptions of inevitability by rejecting the idea that present circumstances result from inexorable, irresistible forces, such as the logic of industrialization or modernization. Instead, if the history of social policy has a moral, it lies in the realization that policies and institutions that appear oppressive today are built in significant measure of human agency and choice. One goal of studying the past is not to be trapped by history but to transcend it.

Not only do I resolutely refuse to offer concrete solutions, I do not try to advance a systematic theory of welfare-state development or of the relations between education and society. My conviction as a historian is that all grand theories simplify and distort by imposing a false consistency on the past. Social institutions have served multiple, often contradictory purposes; coalitions with widely divergent interests and goals have sponsored reform and policy. The story of American social policy has identifiable themes and recurrent patterns. Still, like all history, it is messy (messier than I can describe in synthetic essays), full of ironies and inconsistencies, but nonetheless powerful and important for everyone who cares about the great unresolved social issues haunting America today.

The first three of this book's four chapters focus on the history of policy. They emphasize the protean definition of *public* and *private*, the influence of the structure of government on the development of social institutions, the complex associations of race, gender, and class with policy, and ideas about the role of government and the sources of poverty that, over and over again throughout American history, have led to attempts to solve social problems by changing the behavior of poor people. Each chapter begins autobiographically, with a short account of my involvement in the issues—welfare reform, the underclass debate, urban school reform—and explains how history has proved essential to their interpretation. Each chapter illustrates the interpretive power of history by focusing on a strand in social policy in the nineteenth and twentieth centuries: social welfare from the poorhouse era through the New Deal; characterizations about those suffering from urban poverty as the undeserving poor to the underclass; the emergence of public education through the radical school reform movement now at work in Chicago.

In each chapter, I consider the implications of the story for confronting major questions of social policy today. The book concludes by shifting its perspective from policy makers and reformers to poor people themselves. Chapter 4 explains the origins of my interest in restoring agency and dignity to ordinary historical actors and asks how poor people have survived poverty. It suggests answers by drawing on the lives of some of the poorest people in early-twentieth-century New York City.

Central to the three focuses of this book—history, contemporary social issues, and personal experience—is a concentration on process.

More than a set of stories about the past, "history" signifies an episte-
mology; through constructing narratives that order experience into
processes that occur over time, people explain everything from the
mundane aspects of daily life to the great social institutions that chan-
nel their experience. Without unraveling the processes through which
they emerged, for example, it is impossible to explain the current features of welfare, education, or inner-city poverty. The same holds for
intellectual agendas, which grow out of the logic of disciplines, the
personal experience of scholars, and the climate of the times—and my
own intellectual agenda, as this book makes clear, is no exception.

All written history is part autobiography. In the recent history of
social institutions and policy, the personal elements of scholarship
become both more visible and troubling. Few historians devote years
to the study of education, mental illness, poverty, crime, cities, civil
rights, or gender unless they care passionately about them. However
careful their research and measured their language, their social com-
mitments shine through their writing. These histories raise questions
about the conventional boundaries of scholarship. As part of their
professionalization project in the early-twentieth century, social scientists rejected the association of research with "advocacy" character-
istic of an earlier generation of scholars, and constructed, in its place,
a concept of "objectivity" that became the hallmark of professionalism. Nonetheless, questions remained unresolved. Where, exactly, is
the border between advocacy and objectivity? Who is entitled to police it?[1]

Throughout their professional lives, those historians who straddle
the border between advocacy and objectivity uneasily, sometimes in-
consistently, find themselves caught between passion and professionalism. Why do some historians choose this often uncomfortable, con-
flict-filled road strewn with rigid critics who doubt the legitimacy of
the questions that drive their scholarship and deny their professionalism? In this book, I have tried to answer this question about myself
explicitly, if not completely, by explaining something of the odyssey

[1] The phrase is borrowed from Mary O. Furner, *Advocacy and Objectivity: A Crisis in
the Professionalization of American Social Science* (Lexington: University of Kentucky
Press, 1975).

that has led this historian to the stories of poor people in America's cities and to the histories of the institutions that have served them. The story begins at the end of my undergraduate years with the almost accidental process through which I became a social historian.

.　.　.　.　.

In 1961, I intended to study for a doctorate in American intellectual history. A senior majoring in history and literature at Harvard, I wanted to go to Berkeley to work with Henry May. At Harvard, the two great intellectual influences on me had been Perry Miller and Oscar Handlin. Miller dominated American history and literature. His majestic work not only rescued the New England Puritans from the charge of anti-intellectual bigotry, it pointed toward a coherent intellectual tradition throughout American history. Through its passion and brilliance it also conveyed the excitement of ideas in history. For me, Miller shone most brightly not in his written work but in his course on American Romanticism, offered (for the only time, I believe) during my senior year and never adequately represented in his writing. Handlin also influenced me most through a course, his year-long survey of American social history, although *Boston's Immigrants* and *The Uprooted* were among the most important books I read as an undergraduate. My senior thesis, a social analysis of Boston's reaction to the Mexican War, reflected Handlin's empirical approach more than Miller's outlook, but in history and literature circles, Miller clearly had greater glamour, and I wanted to study ideas. In retrospect, I am struck by the narrow vision underlying American history and literature at Harvard and the American Studies movement of the time. Not only did they omit women and African Americans, they remained preoccupied with a central question—What accounts for the uniqueness of America?—without examining the assumptions on which it rested.

The fellowship Berkeley offered me wasn't large enough to bring my family (wife, two children) across the continent and support us in California. Graduate school, at least for the time, appeared out of the question. The alternative was making money. From my experience as an encyclopedia salesman, my major form of financial aid, I knew I could sell. So, depressed, unshaven, I went one afternoon to Lamont Library to look through books of corporate job listings. Would I do better selling soap or advertising it?

My friend Dan Fox, a graduate student in history, happened to come by the reading room. I told him my dilemma. He asked if I had heard about the Master of Arts in Teaching Program at the Harvard Graduate School of Education. The School of Education? Teaching? No, I had not heard of the program or ever thought of the School of Education as a possibility. Dan explained that the program allowed students to take half their courses in a discipline, was looking for graduates of Ivy League schools with good grades, and had a lot of money for financial support in the form of internships as well as fellowships. One could enroll, take a number of history courses, then enter a Ph.D. program in history the following year.

The idea seemed worth at least looking into. Even a school of education held more appeal than Procter and Gamble or J. Walter Thompson. Walking for the first time in my four years at Harvard into Lawrence Hall, then the home of the School of Education, I found the admissions office and asked for literature on the M.A.T. program. To my shock, a secretary showed me into the office of the assistant dean, Frank Duhay, who started to interview me. Why, he asked, did I want to go into high school teaching? Because the idea had not occurred to me more than an hour earlier, answering him required some invention. Uncomfortable with the plausible tale I had begun to spin, I stopped in the middle. I told him I wanted to go to graduate school and needed money. Could he help? He wanted to know my grades. I told him and he asked how much I needed.

Harvard's Graduate School of Education (HGSE) proved an extraordinary place. The M.A.T. year began with an intense summer program. Four of us with two master teachers were to teach the history of the world (defined as Europe since 1789) to Newton junior high school students in six weeks. We taught in the morning, criticized each other and planned the next day's lessons in the early afternoon, staggered back for classes at Harvard a few days a week, and prepared at night. In retrospect, the arrogance with which I started was appalling. Luckily, it didn't survive very long. Teaching, I imagined, should be easy because I knew a lot of history. How difficult could it be to tell kids about it? As it turned out, teaching, as my critics drove home, was very hard, harder than anything I'd ever done, and the master teachers, high school teachers during the regular academic year, knew a lot more history than I did and they knew, as well, how to convey it to adolescents. By the end of the summer I had been hooked. What career line I would follow wasn't clear, but it wouldn't be as a conventional historian.

The M.A.T. program left me confused about my career path. The easiest route would be to stay in graduate school and do something connected with education. But what? Fortunately, the award of a traveling fellowship to England allowed me to postpone the decision for a year. I had thought I would study how social studies was taught in British schools, but in the summer of 1962 one of the accidents that shape the process through which careers are formed intervened. A transformative experience working with poor children and their parents in a settlement house (described in chapter 4) altered my plans and, in important ways, my life. I now wanted to study relations between education and the working class, to focus on the links between cities, poverty, and children.

I returned from England admitted to the doctoral program in HGSE but unable to decide what my focus there should be. One evening in early September, shortly before classes were to start, I walked home with the dean, Theodore Sizer, who was my adviser. Ted had a doctorate in history and had taught a seminar in the history of education that I had taken during my M.A.T. year. He said (I am paraphrasing), "Why don't you go into the history of education? You have the background; you know how to do historical research. History gives you great flexibility. People seem to like to hire historians as administrators." I took his advice.

Based in a school of education, my graduate training took a very different form than it would have had I been in the history department. I read less political and diplomatic history, but in Daniel Calhoun I found a superb mentor who pushed me toward analytic social history and forced me to use a computer in historical analysis years before quantification had become more common among conventional historians. At the same time, an array of instructive experiences taught me about matters other than history: supervising student teachers; studying philosophy of education with Israel Scheffler and working as one of his assistants when he chaired a committee that wrote a comprehensive report on the future of HGSE; serving on the editorial board of the *Harvard Educational Review* and as an assistant to sociologist Robert Dreeben when he was writing his important book, *On What Is Learned in School*, which has influenced the way I have thought about schools in the past as well as the present; and simply talking every day with the teaching fellows who shared office cubicles on the top floor of Longfellow Hall (where the School of Education had moved), only one of whom, as I recall, also was a historian.

This intense, eclectic education left me impatient with conventional disciplinary boundaries, at ease in interdisciplinary settings, searching for ways to link scholarship and social action. Nonetheless, I thought that my dissertation topic, an exploration of the links among urban-industrial development, social class, and the origins of public education in Massachusetts, while relevant to my larger intellectual agenda, remained firmly anchored in the past.

Thinking I had finished, I handed Ted Sizer and Dan Calhoun an absurdly long version consisting of several case studies linked together only by a common focus on a time and place. They summoned me to Ted's office, where they told me that although each of the case studies was interesting, the dissertation had no theme or argument. I should decide what it said, rewrite, and then return. In retrospect, it is still hard for me to understand why I remained unable to see the larger themes in the dissertation or to see its relation to current school-reform debates. The intellectual effect of prolonged immersion in detailed data accounts for some of the myopia, I am sure. I have seen the same effect often with my graduate students; the cliché about the forest and the trees rings true (or, as a more arresting statement brought me by a graduate student years later when I was drowning in quantitative data read, "When you are up to your ass in alligators, it is hard to remind yourself that your initial objective was to drain the swamp").

I think, though, that something more was going on. Based in the school of education, I was determined to prove my legitimacy as a real historian. I wanted my dissertation to be rigorous and professional. Somewhere deep inside, I probably was afraid to move very far from the data about the past. Far more than I realized, my own ideas about scholarly legitimacy had been shaped in a context that accepted the dichotomy between pure and applied research and treated disciplinary boundaries as real, rather than as convenient fictions created for the most part when knowledge was institutionalized in modern universities in the late-nineteenth and early-twentieth centuries. Even a school of education had left me unable to transgress these boundaries without a sense of fraudulence.

As a consequence, I looked for the frame of my dissertation in social science, not in the links between past and present. The problem was the poverty of the social science literature, especially on the role of education in economic development and modernization. Nothing I read seemed capable of providing an intellectual frame for the whole. The most interesting social science for my purposes was Leon Festinger's concept of cognitive dissonance, which helped explain some of the reformers' actions but hardly could encompass the entire story.

For some months I read rather aimlessly, wandered around a lot, and worried. Sensing I was moving nowhere fast, Dan Calhoun sat me down one morning and handed me a list of items. This, he said, is what I think you are saying. With a few revisions and some rewording, he was right, and in a few weeks I rewrote the dissertation, which became *The Irony of Early School Reform*, published in 1968. What Dan had showed me was that, without realizing it, I had written about the links between past and present, that I was using history to interpret contemporary educational reform.

When I finished my dissertation in 1966, I thought of myself as a serious professional historian. Nonetheless, my ambivalence remained far from resolved, and when Dan Fox, now director of field operations for the Appalachian volunteers in Berea, Kentucky, invited me down to talk about a job, I went eagerly. For a number of reasons, I chose, in the end, an academic career, although not one completely in the mainstream. I went to a new institution, the Ontario Institute for Studies in Education, affiliated with the University of Toronto, then in

15

its second year, where I could write and teach the history of education, help pioneer the study of modern social history in English-speaking Canada, and contribute to the building of an interdisciplinary social science setting for the study of education. In Toronto, I continued work on the history of urban education, especially the origins of bureaucracy. *The Irony of Early School Reform* had examined the origins of urban public education using social structure as its primary lens. Now I decided to substitute organizations as the main lens. This led me to reimagine the origins of public education as a competition among organizational forms and to analyze its subsequent institutionalization as a classic case of bureaucratization. (The essays exploring these perspectives appear in *Class, Bureaucracy, and Schools* and, in revised form, in *Reconstructing American Education.*)

While working on urban education, I also began a long-term project reconstructing the population of a Canadian city (Hamilton, Ontario) during its early industrialization. The Canadian city project started as an attempt to remedy a weakness in my earlier work on education, the failure to provide an empirical foundation for the assertions about class and social structure on which a number of my interpretations had rested. With quantitative data from one city (later compared to Buffalo, New York), the project reconstructed the intricate relations among occupation, wealth, gender, age, ethnicity, property ownership, social mobility, family organization, and the life course during the emergence of industrial capitalism. (Its primary results appear in *The People of Hamilton, Canada West* and *The Social Organization of Early Industrial Capitalism*, written with my two close collaborators in the research, Michael Doucet and Mark Stern.) Nonetheless, trying to build a rigorous, engaged social history proved a task full of irony. With what always has seemed to me a shallow, mistaken disdain, many historians on the political Left rejected quantification as an inherently bourgeois, antihumanistic tool diverting history from its proper focus on the lives and struggles of ordinary people or the political power that circumscribed their opportunities. In reality, quantification permitted historians to recover, describe, and interpret the lives of common folk, to write history from the bottom up, with unprecedented detail, accuracy, and scope. It enabled them, as well, to describe the emergence of class structures and the powerful, persisting influence of class, gender, and race on social relations and opportunity structures. Quantitative data also rendered unmistakable the contextual, socially constructed aspects of family forms and phases in the life course, such as adolescence. My failure to help build wide and sturdy bridges between historians with similar intellectual projects but different methods remains one of my greatest professional disappointments, and one that has diminished the quality of scholarship in both camps.

By the mid-1970s, I began to think about new research directions. I wanted to combine my earlier interest in the history of institutions with the quantitative study of populations represented in the Canadian city project. The analysis of institutional demography seemed the answer. Histories of asylums, reformatories, and prisons for the most part concentrated on the ideas of reformers and administrators, on legislation, and on administrative practices. Almost no one had written about inmates: who they were, what led them to incarceration, what influence they exerted on institutions. Did the sources exist for a history of institutions from the bottom up? To answer the question, I spent a summer wandering around some of the archives in New York State and found more than enough material for a lifetime of work.

Selecting a sample of the available records, I secured funding from the National Institute for Mental Health for a project reconstructing institutional demography, using poorhouse registers, pauper surveys, and census material. As the work progressed, my focus broadened from demography to the issue of dependence in America's past, which historians had not treated adequately. How had dependence been defined? What were its sources? Why were some people unable to care for themselves? How had they been treated by public policy and private charity? Did similar assumptions guide ideas and policy for different categories of dependent people? In *Poverty and Policy in American History*, I explored answers to these questions.

Research for the book had turned up wonderful primary sources illustrating ideas about poverty and welfare in the nineteenth century. With two colleagues, Susan Davis and Mark Stern, I proposed to Steven Fraser at Basic Books a little volume illustrating the continuity

17

and parallels in ideas about these issues between past and present. Although he liked the idea, Steve said that authored books about a topic carried more impact than edited collections and suggested we write a social history of American social welfare. Not realizing the size of the task, we agreed; the result became *In the Shadow of the Poorhouse* (for a variety of reasons, with me as the author).

Throughout the years of working on the first two books on poverty and welfare, I was waiting impatiently to turn to an extraordinary collection, case histories from the New York Charity Organization Society, which would be the basis for a detailed exploration of the experience of poverty in the late-nineteenth and early-twentieth centuries. In the course of talking with Andre Schiffrin and Sara Bershtel of Pantheon Books about the project, they described a new series on the politics of knowledge and invited me to write a short book for it on poverty. The opportunity seemed too intriguing to pass up. Again, underestimating the job, I agreed. Within a couple of years, though, I had become depressed about the project. The literature seemed stale; authors repackaged the same ideas over and over again. I could produce my own version, but it hardly seemed worth the effort. One day, suddenly, I realized that the tired, repetitive quality of the literature itself signified the problem that needed a history. The question became how to identify and account for the core ideas running throughout two centuries of comment on poverty and welfare, how to explain the inability to move thinking out of worn and unproductive grooves. With this realization, a new plan for the book that became *The Undeserving Poor* took shape.

There has been both an accidental quality and an underlying coherence in the paths I have followed. As with most people, my own experience encapsulates the mix of accident, process, and pattern that constitutes the history of individuals as well as institutions, societies, or nations. In my case, although each project has led to the next in often unpredictable, obscure ways, each has tried to use history to offer something of interest to social theory or to the interpretation of major social issues and institutions. This book synthesizes some of these explorations.

The Welfare State

LATE IN 1992, Governor Robert Casey of Pennsylvania appointed me to his Task Force on Reducing Welfare Dependency. I had written a book on the social history of welfare as well as one on ideas about poverty in recent American history and, for several years, had co-chaired an interdisciplinary faculty–graduate student seminar on work and welfare that had discussed current research and major policy issues. From the seminar I had learned of the disappointing results of much current welfare reform and the ambiguous results of research as well as of a few promising innovations sponsored by both governments and not-for-profit agencies. From my historical research, I knew that welfare reform usually served as a synonym for cutting benefits to poor people. Reducing welfare dependency usually has not meant setting people on the road to independence through education, a living wage, and good job prospects. Rather, it has referred to strategies for bumping people off welfare rolls and into low-wage, dead-end, temporary jobs or onto the streets. To be sure, exceptions exist, but they represent a minority among "reforms." Would this task force be any different? By serving, would I be participating in one more mean hoax played on poor people? By declining to serve, would I be shirking a civic duty, missing an opportunity to contribute even a tiny amount—and what did a historian have to offer?—to some incremental gain for those Pennsylvanians most in need?

Around the country, state legislatures had been enacting punitive welfare reforms, penalizing parents for their children's poor school attendance, limiting benefits when women on welfare gave birth to a third child, requiring teenage mothers to live with their parents. Similar proposals had surfaced in the Pennsylvania legislature the previous spring, and the governor had appointed the Task Force to study the issues. Even if the Task Force offered few positive suggestions, at the least it might help prevent Pennsylvania from repeating the his-

19

toric equation of welfare reform with reducing benefits that was sweeping the country.

The arguments for joining the Task Force proved compelling. Besides, I was intrigued. This was as close as I had come to the actual world of policy and politics. It was a chance to glimpse from the inside what historians write about from a distance. As it happened, the Task Force, although limited by a narrow charge and meager prospects for new resources, explicitly refused to equate reform with cutting benefits and produced a moderately progressive document (which, unfortunately, has had only a minimal impact on subsequent state legislation).[1] Its members, drawn from business, not-for-profits, trade unions, advocates, former welfare recipients, the legislature, and universities worked hard, seriously, and reached, to me anyway, surprising consensus. How did this group—so diverse on every dimension—reach agreement?

The answer rests in members' shared dislike of welfare. For his or her own reasons, everyone started out as a critic of welfare. The more we learned about how the system discouraged independence and degraded its recipients, the more appalled members became. (I recall seeing, for the first time, the application form required for welfare in Pennsylvania; my first reactions were that it was more complicated than the college applications my daughter had filled out recently and that I'd be tempted to steal before subjecting myself to it.)

In their dislike of welfare, Task Force members reflected the nearly universal views of Americans. No other major social institution evokes such hostility from its clients, who find it punitive and degrading, from liberals, who see it as hopelessly inadequate and full of disincentives, or from conservatives, who believe it is overly generous and rewards bad behavior. Nor are these views new. They echo historic attacks on poor laws in the late-eighteenth and nineteenth centuries. In one way or another, they have reverberated through criticism of America's incomplete welfare state since its founding legislation in the 1930s. In 1994, they underlay President Bill Clinton's goal of "ending welfare as we know it."

[1] *Governor's Task Force to Reduce Welfare Dependency*, Final Report (Harrisburg, Penn., 1993).

How remarkable, then, that welfare has remained so impervious to real reform. What accounts for the inability of the people in this rich, inventive country to create and implement policies that adequately support with dignity those among us in need? To encourage and help them to find the resources for the independent lives almost all of them want? Here is a serious puzzle on which historians can shed at least some light.

Real welfare reform is partly a problem of interests and politics, partly a problem of ideology. Welfare has served a series of mixed, sometimes conflicting interests that inhibit reform, while debates about welfare reflect a set of historic preoccupations and stale ideas about poor people that discourage fresh thought. In one way or another, welfare reform (including many of the state initiatives in the early 1990s) has been as much about improving poor people by changing their behavior as about helping them with food, housing, or cash. At the same time, mythical images of a golden era of voluntarism have undermined attempts to formulate public policy that could unleash the capacity of government in constructive ways. Indeed, like Presidents Ronald Reagan and George Bush, a great many Americans believe that once-upon-a-time Americans took care of their needy through private means and that government welfare is un-American.

Social scientists often share and reinforce these mythical views of welfare's past. Several years ago, I heard an economic historian argue that American history lacked the debates over poor laws that raged so fiercely in late-eighteenth- and early-nineteenth-century Britain. Until I had worked in the primary sources myself, I would have agreed with him. From reading the standard secondary sources, one only could assume the insignificance of public relief (the old term for welfare) in America's past. In fact, this conclusion is wrong. American debates and policies often paralleled those in Britain, and public assistance always has relieved a great many dependent people. Failure to grasp the role of public welfare in America's past today fuels nostalgia for a nonexistent age of pure voluntarism and raises unrealistic expectations for the capacity of private action to ameliorate public problems.

21

Nonetheless, the boundaries between public and private welfare practice in America's past remain ambiguous and elusive. Indeed, until well into the nineteenth century, "public" did not signify institutions or practices both financed and administered by government, and strategies for carrying out social tasks blended government, philanthropic, and personal resources in a variety of ways. As a result, American welfare, or relief as it was known until the twentieth century, always had a mixed economy.

In this chapter, I sketch the history of this mixed economy. I concentrate on one dimension of the public/private relation: the role of governmental and nongovernmental sources in the funding and provision of social welfare. I do not consider the implications of "private," defined as activity within domestic or family settings. This chapter is, moreover, old-fashioned history because of its from-the-top-down story. It describes the formulation and implementation of policy for poor and otherwise needy people. The complete story regards events from the perspective of clients; it views welfare provision as a complicated, obstacle-strewn terrain, not usefully regarded as either public or private, negotiated by people in need of help using their own intelligence and strategies.[2] In chapter 4, I give some examples of how families survived extreme poverty earlier in this century.

This chapter is also incomplete because it touches only marginally on the history of elementary and secondary education. However, education has constituted one of the key public benefits provided by governments since the nineteenth century. As such, it has been a fundamental strategy in state responses to poverty, crime, alleged family inadequacy, and the requirements of economic growth. No account of the welfare state is complete without its inclusion, and I discuss its

[2] Michael B. Katz, "Families and Welfare: A Philadelphia Case," in *Poverty and Policy in American History* (New York: Academic Press, 1983); "The History of an Impudent Poor Woman in New York City from 1918 to 1923," in Peter Mandler, ed., *The Uses of Charity: The Poor on Relief in the Nineteenth-Century Metropolis* (Philadelphia: University of Pennsylvania Press, 1990), pp. 227–46; "Surviving Poverty in Early Twentieth Century New York," in Arnold Hirsch and Ray Mohl, eds., *History and Twentieth-Century Urban Policy* (New Brunswick, N.J.: Rutgers University Press, 1993), which has been adapted as chapter 4 of this book.

history in chapter 3 of this book. (The case for including education as part of the history of social welfare in America is made in the brilliant book *Schooling for All*, by Ira Katznelson and Margaret Weir.)[3]

THE STRUCTURE AND GOALS OF AMERICAN WELFARE

In the seventeenth century, the colonists transposed the Elizabethan Poor Laws, with their pattern of decentralized, tax-supported assistance, to the New World. Public poor relief, therefore, is one of America's oldest traditions, and its local base became one of its enduring features.[4] Throughout American history, poor-relief practice varied not only among states but from county to county within the same state. Even the new federal role, which began in the 1930s and extended in the 1960s, only could modify but not eliminate the local variation in welfare practice, as the persistence of wide differences in Aid to Families with Dependent Children (AFDC) benefits among states reveals. In 1980, a Mississippi single-parent family of four received, at most, $120 in monthly AFDC benefits, compared to more than $500 in New York or California. Local control (now primarily at the state, rather than the town or county, level) thus remains one historic, structural feature of American welfare.

The bifurcation between public assistance and social insurance constitutes a second enduring structural feature of American welfare. Public assistance refers to means-tested relief given only to those whose resources fall below a certain standard. Social insurance, by contrast, is not means tested. It is an entitlement for everyone eligible by virtue of fixed, objective criteria such as age, disability, or unemployment. Throughout American history, the public assistance model

[3] Ira Katznelson and Margaret Weir, *Schooling for All: Class, Race, and the Decline of the Democratic Ideal* (New York: Basic Books, 1985).

[4] This chapter draws principally on some of my books. Unless otherwise noted, full documentation of the points here can be found in them. They are: *Poverty and Policy in American History* (New York: Academic Press, 1983); *In the Shadow of the Poorhouse: A Social History of Welfare in America* (New York: Basic Books, 1986); *Reconstructing American Education* (Cambridge: Harvard University Press, 1987); *The Undeserving Poor: From the War on Poverty to the War on Welfare* (New York: Pantheon, 1990). I have footnoted only direct quotations and other material not documented in the books.

dominated poor relief, and social insurance developed only in the twentieth century. Today, public assistance is what we call welfare, and its major form is AFDC; the great example of social insurance, of course, is Social Security.

Two points about this division between social insurance and public assistance require emphasis. First, it was not inevitable. Early social insurance advocates hoped for a unified and coherent system embracing all forms of social welfare. Not until the New Deal in the 1930s did public policy firmly embed the distinction into the structure of America's welfare system. After the New Deal years, subsequent legislation combined with the deliberate policy of the Social Security Administration to widen and solidify the emergent distinction between social insurance and public assistance. In the process, *welfare* became just another euphemism for *relief*.

As a result, American social welfare contains a class and gender structure. Social insurance serves nearly everyone. Its base of support cuts across class lines, and much of its constituency is articulate and vigorous. Indeed, the militancy of the middle-class elderly pushed old-age insurance to the top of the New Deal's social agenda and, nearly five decades later, defeated President Ronald Reagan's plans to trim benefits. However, its insurance ideology notwithstanding, Social Security remains an income-transfer program whose supporters obscure its similarities to what, derisively, Americans call welfare. Welfare, which is for poor people, inherits the mantle of poor relief, and those who depend on it lack both the political power to extend its benefits and the social status to erase its historic stigma. As a consequence, Social Security now lifts most elderly people out of poverty; AFDC almost never does the same for the single parents with children who are its primary clients. Between 1970 and 1985, the average Social Security benefit increased 400 percent; the average AFDC benefit rose only 50 percent.

The division between AFDC and the social insurance programs, Linda Gordon has argued, incorporated into the structure of the welfare state the gendered distinctions embedded in social thought about poverty, risk, and dependence. "The social insurance programs developed from an almost exclusively male current of thought, while public assistance developed from an integrated perspective, with the advice of many female leaders."[5] Gordon has in mind primarily the mothers' pensions introduced in many states after 1911 and the work of the women in the federal Children's Bureau who supported their extension and incorporation into national legislation in the 1930s. Although female public officials and reformers played a leading role in the formulation of the Aid to Dependent Children (ADC) provision of the Economic Security Act of 1935 (the original Social Security legislation), which drew on the model of experience of mothers' pensions, public assistance emerged from a much older practice, public outdoor relief, which was devised and administered by men. Nonetheless, most recipients of outdoor relief and subsequent forms of public assistance have been women. By contrast, social insurance, in Theda Skocpol's terms, reflected a patriarchal model of welfare that disproportionately directed benefits to male family heads, leaving problems distinctive to women either uncovered or relegated to public assistance, whose much lower benefits often have been administered in more intrusive ways. Within the world of public assistance, however, women have fared better than men. Aside from food stamps, the only public assistance for single men comes from state-run General Assistance programs, whose benefits, in recent years attacked and reduced in many states, remain far lower than those paid by AFDC.[6]

A third structural feature of American welfare also has a long history. Political theorist Alan Wolfe has termed it America's "franchise state," and it is one product of the blurred boundary between public and private in America, which will be illustrated in the pages that follow.[7] By franchise state, Wolfe means that governments utilize pri-

[5] Linda Gordon, "Social Insurance and Public Assistance: The Influence of Gender in Welfare Thought in the United States, 1890–1935," *American Historical Review* 97:1 (February 1992): 20.

[6] Robyn Muncy, *Creating a Female Dominion in American Reform, 1890–1935* (New York: Oxford University Press, 1991); Theda Skocpol, *Protecting Soldiers and Mothers: The Political Origins of Social Policy in the United States* (Cambridge: Harvard University Press, 1992).

[7] Alan Wolfe, *The Limits of Legitimacy: Political Contradictions of Contemporary Capitalism* (New York: Free Press, 1975), pp. 108–75; this argument is also made forcefully by Lester M. Salamon, "The Nonprofit Sector and Government: The American Experience in Theory and Practice," in Helmut K. Anheier and Wolfgang Seibel, eds., *The Third*

SCHAUMBURG TWP. DISTRICT LIBRARY

vate agencies or firms to accomplish public purposes. Throughout the nineteenth century, for instance, state governments paid voluntary associations and religious groups to manage orphanages and institutions for most classes of dependent people. In the 1960s, federal government support for social services, delivered largely through "private" agencies, expanded enormously. For example, from 1965 to 1980, federal expenses for education, training, employment, and social services increased from 1.9 to 5.9 percent of the federal budget, or about 300 percent. In 1981, government provided 41 percent of the income of nonprofit human service agencies.[8] Most private agencies probably depend on governments for at least half their operating incomes, and as their independence has declined, their role has changed. Voluntary agencies have become primarily service providers, not innovators.

Supply-side policies always have dominated relief and welfare in America. This is their fourth structural feature. Public policy has tried to reduce poverty by changing the behavior of poor people, for example, by frightening them with poorhouses, threatening to take away their children, training them in new skills, or regulating their sexuality. Public policy, however, has done little to address the reasons why so many young, healthy people (especially women with children) continue to find themselves in poverty; why one of four Americans falls below the poverty line for some point during the course of a decade; or why pretransfer poverty (that is, the proportion of individuals in poverty before they received government income support) has not declined in more than twenty-five years.[9]

A fifth structural feature of American welfare is much newer: its extension of benefits to a wide and diverse segment of the American

---

Sector: Comparative Studies of Nonprofit Organizations (Berlin: Walter de Gruyter, 1990), pp. 222–26.

[8] Salamon, "The American Experience," p. 225, table 4; Ralph M. Kramer, *Voluntary Agencies in the Welfare State* (Berkeley and Los Angeles: University of California Press, 1981), is a good overview of trends.

[9] Greg J. Duncan, *Years of Poverty, Years of Plenty: The Changing Fortunes of American Workers and Families* (Ann Arbor: Institute for Social Research, University of Michigan, 1984); June Axinn and Mark J. Stern, *Dependency and Poverty: Old Problems in a New World* (Lexington, Mass.: Lexington Books, 1988), pp. 64, 83.

population. According to one expert, "by 1980 . . . over 80 percent of poor households and 45 percent of all households received a cash or in-kind transfer in that year."[10] The poorest fifth of the population receive at least half their income from the federal government. They depend, now, as much on the government as on the labor market. Between 1965 and 1980, the share of the federal budget spent on income security, social services, and health, education, training, and employment increased from 27 to 53 percent. Between 1968 and 1978, about one of every four Americans lived in a family that received welfare (*excluding* Social Security, veterans' pensions, and medical assistance) during the decade. This wide diffusion of benefits, which dates from the latter 1960s, resulted from a variety of sources. Some were demographic: the growing proportion of elderly people and single-parent families. Some stemmed from program participation: the massive increase in the proportion of eligible families claiming AFDC in the late 1960s. And some reflected policy: for example, administrative changes in eligibility standards, the transformation of the food stamp program in the late 1960s, the passage of Medicare and Medicaid in 1965, and the melding of programs into Supplemental Social Security in 1972.

Despite its expansion between roughly 1965 and 1980, America's social welfare system remains incomplete. This forms another structural feature. As everyone knows, America remains (as of this writing in the summer of 1994) the only major Western country without national health insurance or a system of family allowances. Among industrial democracies, only Japan spends less of its gross national product on social welfare. More than one of every five children in America lives in poverty. In infant mortality, America ranks seventeenth among Western nations. The rate for blacks, 17.6 per 100,000 (compared to 8.5 per 100,000 for whites), is more similar to the rate for people living in the Third World than in other modern, developed nations.[11]

[10] Robert Haveman, *Poverty Policy and Poverty Research: The Great Society and the Social Sciences* (Madison: University of Wisconsin Press, 1987), p. 28.

[11] William P. O'Hare, Kevin M. Pollard, and Taynia L. Mann, *African Americans in the 1990s*, Population Bulletin 46, 1 (Washington, D.C.: Population Reference Bureau, July 1991), pp. 13–14.

America's economy remains unable to check the forces that generate poverty, and its social welfare system cannot alleviate many of its consequences. Almost everyone recognizes the gaps, weaknesses, and disincentives of the current system, but fundamental change has proved elusive. Why has this irrational and unsatisfactory system proved so resistant to change? The answer lies in a combination of the persistence of its historic purposes, the ideas on which it rests, and the interests it serves. Chapter 2 will describe ideas about poverty underpinning relief and welfare throughout American history. The discussion that follows in this chapter highlights welfare's purposes and the interests it has served.

Neither public nor private, American relief and welfare practice have served multiple, sometimes conflicting purposes. Four of these date to the early-nineteenth century, the fifth to the 1960s. Relief's first historic goal always has been the alleviation of distress: the prevention of death by starvation, homelessness, lack of clothing, and disease. At the same time, public officials and private employers have used relief to regulate labor markets by controlling the supply and price of labor through manipulating incentives to work.

The impact of income support on the supply and cost of labor is the most ancient and enduring issue in discourse about poverty and welfare. Will welfare erode the will to work? Will overly generous relief policies force a rise in wages? Who will accept a hard, boring, badly paid job if welfare is an option? Always, the doctrine of less eligibility has governed relief and welfare policy. Benefits never should match or exceed the standard of living attainable by those working for the lowest ordinary wages. These concerns helped prompt new poor laws in the early-nineteenth century that tried to make incarceration in a poorhouse the price for help. In the third quarter of the nineteenth century, they underlay the new Scientific Charity Movement's harsh attempts to evaluate male applicants for relief by compelling them to submit to a work test, usually chopping wood or breaking stone. In the twentieth century, southern agricultural interests fought to keep state welfare benefits low, objected to the wages paid by relief programs in the New Deal, and retarded the extension of Social Security to farmworkers. Welfare's potential impact on work incentives stimulated the expensive and inconclusive guaranteed income experiments of the 1960s and 1970s and framed debates about income support programs. Concern with work incentives also has driven the current enthusiasm for "workfare."

Along with reformers, public officials and employers have deployed relief to improve poor people by regulating behavior as a weapon in the endless war against drink, shiftlessness, and sex. At times, welfare has served to dampen or forestall militancy among workers who might riot or join together in powerful political movements. These concerns motivated some of the Progressive Era industrialists who developed programs known as *welfare capitalism*, for instance. Moral anxieties also have fueled welfare policy throughout American history because reformers often have located the source of poverty in the character and behavior of the poor, as chapter 2 will describe in some detail. In the nineteenth century, reformers hoped poorhouses would frighten paupers out of their drunkenness and sloth. In the South in the 1940s and 1950s, allegations about the sexual behavior of black women stimulated the use of "suitable home" provisions in Aid to Dependent Children regulations.[12] In the 1990s, concerns about the sexuality of teenagers and mothers on welfare drive recommendations for punitive reforms throughout the country.

Relief and welfare also have been potent catalysts of political mobilization, motivating not only campaigns by those who have sought their benefits but crusades against them by opponents. Indeed, opposition to public welfare has helped carry more than one aspiring politician to office. Relief and welfare always have been part of the patronage apparatus through which politicians have garnered votes. In the nineteenth century, local politicians used relief policies not only to win the votes of the poor but to appeal to small businessmen and local professionals. Contracts for supplying poorhouses with food and fuel enriched local merchants. Orders for food redeemable at local stores helped support grocers. Cash relief often found its way to saloon keepers. Contracts for medical care augmented the income of local doctors. In the 1930s, welfare policy became one way the New

[12] Winifred Bell, *Aid to Dependent Children* (New York: Columbia University Press, 1965).

Deal lured black voters away from the Republican Party and, subsequently, helped cement the allegiance of minorities and the urban poor to the Democrats. Indeed, in 1963, President Kennedy told Walter Heller, then chairman of the Council of Economic Advisers, that political imperatives demanded a program targeted directly at the poor, partly because the recent tax cut had helped only the middle class. Conversely, opposition to relief and welfare also has persisted as a means for mobilizing support. In the 1870s, Brooklyn's Republican reformers capitalized on the graft that infected the city's welfare system not only to abolish outdoor relief but to ride to political power. The new mayor, Seth Low, later also mayor of New York City and president of Columbia University, was only one of a series of politicians to ride the antiwelfare wave to high political office, as we have witnessed in much more recent times.

In the 1960s, welfare acquired a new purpose as part of the Civil Rights Movement: to reverse the consequences of racial injustice. The Civil Rights Bill of 1964 and the voting rights legislation of 1965 completed the first phase of the movement's agenda; the Watts Riot in Los Angeles in 1965 peeled away the remaining covers from the anger, despair, and frustration that remained within urban ghettos. In the aftermath of these events, civil rights leaders, including Dr. Martin Luther King Jr., increasingly stressed the connection between discrimination and poverty, and they argued that welfare reform, job creation, and income support were essential to progress for African Americans. Issues of race and economic justice fused, to take one example, in the welfare rights movement, inspired and led by black women. They joined, as well, to help ignite the War on Poverty and sustain its one potentially radical innovation: community action.

Four elements of welfare's historic context have shaped the translation of these multiple purposes into programs and policies. Of paramount importance is the distinctive structure of American government. Here I refer particularly to American federalism and the divisions and tensions among levels of government. Second are class tensions that have accompanied the periodic reconstruction of America's social structure. Third is demography, for race, gender, ethnicity, and age composition powerfully and independently have influenced the character of dependence and public response. Fourth is ideology or political culture, especially the fictive separation of politics and economy, which has reinforced a commitment to the illegitimacy of state intervention in the economy, a distrust of government, and an exaltation of voluntarism.

Given these contexts and multiple purposes, American welfare practices emerged as different from those in European countries in several ways. Not only are benefits less extensive and complete, asserts historian Ellis Hawley, but policy planning itself remains incoherent, retarded by patronage politics that defeat meritocratic administrative reforms; unusually reliant on "subnational units" and "quasi-privatist machinery" to implement and adapt federal policy; and unprotected by "formalized corporate mechanisms" shielding policy from interest groups.[13] No single or monocausal explanation accounts for this distinctive, truncated, often incoherent welfare state. By themselves, neither the logic of industrialism, the shape of the state, the goals of capitalist employers, nor the machinations of liberal bureaucrats explain its emergence and configuration.[14] The story instead is a complex, multifaceted tale that spans most of American history.

THE POORHOUSE ERA

Between the end of the colonial period and the early 1940s, the history of America's response to dependence falls into two major periods, which I call the Poorhouse Era and the Construction of the Semi-welfare State. The Poorhouse Era includes the years from the early-nineteenth century to about 1890. Although policies in this period departed from earlier practices, they reflected their colonial legacy. The result was a distinctive strategy, which reached its peak in the 1870s

[13] Ellis W. Hawley, "Social Policy and the Liberal State in Twentieth-Century America," in Donald T. Critchlow and Ellis W. Hawley, eds., *Federal Social Policy: The Historical Dimension* (University Park: Pennsylvania State University Press, 1988), pp. 117–39.

[14] For an incisive discussion of the weaknesses of prevailing theories of welfare history, see Skocpol, *Protecting Soldiers and Mothers*, pp. 4–40. The most subtle and persuasive assessment of the applicability of various theories to the history of social welfare is in George Steinmetz, *Regulating the Social: A Historical Sociology of the Welfare State and Local Politics in Imperial Germany* (Princeton: Princeton University Press, 1994).

and 1880s, for responding to dependence. Its hallmarks were reliance on institutions, hostility to public outdoor relief, the separation of parents and children, and social control through the personal oversight of the poor by the wealthy. The depression of the 1890s vividly revealed the bankruptcy of this strategy, which gradually moved from the forefront to the backwaters of social policy.

Colonial relief practice copied four principles of British poor laws: public responsibility for the relief of destitution; local finance and administration; legal expectation of support by kin; and special concern with the education of dependent children. In practice, these translated into distinctive methods for providing relief: auctioning the care of the poor to the lowest bidder; contracting for their care without competitive bidding; forcing them into almshouses; and mixing institutional care with outdoor relief. All these methods coexisted throughout the colonies and persisted in varying combinations in most of the new states. Complicating their administration were the ubiquitous settlement laws, which restricted relief to dependent people who met local criteria for "settlement," that is, membership in the community. Local authorities shipped others across parish, town, or county borders, allegedly back to their communities of origin.

In the late-eighteenth century, as migration, economic change, and the formation of a mobile wage-labor class increased the prevalence of poverty, settlement became harder to determine, more expensive to administer, and a constant source of conflict and litigation. Increasingly, too, reformers pointed to the abuses inherent in auctioning and contracting out the care of the poor. Still, outdoor relief remained an inadequate policy because, so contemporaries argued, it raised taxes for poor relief and discouraged the poor from seeking work. As in Britain, reformers sought to eliminate outdoor relief and force all dependent people into poorhouses. In both nations, reformers' emphasis on poorhouses reflected a new belief in the power of institutions to solve social problems through their influence on behavior and character, and they translated their faith in the transformative power of institutions not only into poorhouses but also into mental hospitals, penitentiaries, reformatories, and public schools. Indeed, more dependent people undoubtedly found refuge in new general hospitals, mental institutions, and orphanages than in almshouses, and many more continued to receive outdoor relief. Nonetheless, because they embodied the goals of public policy toward dependence, poorhouses are a fitting symbol for this early era in the history of relief.

By forcing people into institutions, reformers expected to curb the growth of pauperism and cut its expense. They argued that poorhouses would curtail the demand for relief, achieve economies of scale, and partly pay for themselves through inmates' labor. They also expected them to improve the character of the poor by inculcating work habits and reversing their intemperance. At the same time, they argued that poorhouses would eliminate the abuses of the auction and contract system and improve the living conditions and prospects of pauper children.

Like all the new institutions created in the first decades of the nineteenth century, poorhouses failed to meet their goals. Indeed, early institutional histories describe a story of disappointment, disillusionment, and the displacement of purpose from reform to custody. Despite the spread of poorhouses throughout the country, in most places expenses for poor relief increased because the per pauper cost of institutional relief proved much higher than that of outdoor, which, perversely as it appeared to people of the time, continued to grow. Nor could poorhouse managers force their inmates to work productively. Strapped for funds, badly administered, poorhouses failed to classify their inmates or reform their characters, and most of them remained wretched places, unsanitary, spreading disease, often actually run by ungovernable inmates who entered and left at will, undercut by corrupt suppliers and managers, and unsupported by a hostile public. In a short time, these institutions intended to reform the care of the poor emerged as feared and despised instruments of public policy.

Nonetheless, the role of poorhouses fluctuated throughout the nineteenth century. In their early years, poorhouses frequently served entire families as places of temporary refuge; by the 1840s families rarely entered together, and most inmates entered by themselves. Especially among the elderly, far more inmates were men than women, because adult children much more willingly housed their mothers than their fathers. The parents of few inmates, contrary to popular stereotypes, themselves had been paupers. Far more often than in the entire population, adult inmates lacked grown children to care for them; many

33

men were victims of industrial accidents and many women widows. In the early decades of the century, many also were sick or mentally ill, and young unmarried women often used poorhouses as places in which to give birth. Nor did most inmates remain long. Indeed, many remained for only short spells between jobs or during family crises.

Shifts in poorhouse demography reflected public policy. Throughout the nineteenth century, the creation of specialized institutions siphoned off many mentally ill and sick inmates. Starting in the 1870s, laws forbidding the commitment of children over the age of two removed youngsters to orphanages, and various policies over the years progressively excluded young, able-bodied men. As a result, poorhouses emerged by the early-twentieth century primarily as public old-age homes, which never have escaped the stigma of their origins.

Although they had little influence on the demand for relief, poorhouses helped create a new profession. Early superintendents of the poor lacked special training and experience. Isolated, overwhelmed with similar problems, they often welcomed the chance to meet. In New York State, their annual conventions debated policy issues and appointed subcommittees to lobby the legislature. Out of these activities emerged a professional identity embodied in the early-twentieth-century exchange of the title "superintendent of the poor" for "public welfare official."

Throughout the nineteenth and early-twentieth centuries, more poor people received help through outdoor relief than in poorhouses. Few public officials defended this practice; many attacked it, but it remained ubiquitous. Attacks on outdoor relief emphasized its role in demoralizing the poor by eroding their independence, self-respect, and willingness to work. They also stressed its role in increasing public costs and its infection by corrupt local politics.

Indeed, outdoor relief persisted partly because it meshed with the distinctive features of nineteenth-century American politics: early, universal white-male suffrage; the formation of a party system that channeled political activity; the mobilization of political activity in cities by decentralized machines; and high voter turnout. In these circumstances, politicians dependent on diverse constituencies used public resources, including relief, to cement voter loyalty. At the same time, relief appealed not only to poor people but to the local merchants and professionals who served them. Indeed, contracts for coal, supplies for poorhouses, medical care, and the cash or chits with which to purchase food and drink offered a wide field for patronage and graft. Sometimes outdoor relief also sustained local labor supplies because without outdoor relief, vast numbers of seasonal workers thrown out of their jobs in the winter either would migrate or starve, especially in cities that offered few opportunities for married women to offset their husbands' periodic loss of income. Thus, no city that bordered one of the Great Lakes abolished public outdoor relief in the late-nineteenth century, despite the virulent and elsewhere successful campaign against it.

Indeed, during the nineteenth century reformers waged wars against outdoor relief, whose history traced a repeated dialectic of expansion and contraction. The most prominent and successful campaign against it surfaced in the 1870s, led by Seth Low, then an aspiring politician in Brooklyn. Under his leadership, Brooklyn became the first of ten of the nation's forty largest cities to abolish public outdoor relief between the 1870s and the 1890s. Others reduced the amount they provided.

Nineteenth-century government's major role, argues Richard L. McCormick, was resource distribution. Governments served groups of private entrepreneurs through the distribution of the resources and privileges necessary to promote commercial and industrial growth. In parallel fashion, local machines manipulated city governments to serve their own ends, which also included redistributing resources. Using relief, machines aided the petty business classes and the poor through unsanctioned, sometimes illegal channels. Viewed this way, machine politics emerge as less alien to the spirit of American democracy than reformers contended. Although late-nineteenth-century reformers relentlessly attacked policies identified with political machines, outdoor relief persisted because it proved indispensable.[15]

[15] Richard L. McCormick, *The Party Period and Public Policy: American Politics from the Age of Jackson to the Progressive Era* (New York: Oxford University Press, 1986), pp. 204–14. On political machines, see Steven P. Erie, *Rainbow's End: Irish Americans and the Dilemma of Machine Politics* (Berkeley and Los Angeles: University of California Press, 1988); Terrence J. McDonald, *The Parameters of Urban Fiscal Policy: Socioeconomic Change*

The scattered statistics charting the demography of its recipients reveal most of them as widows, sick, elderly, or temporarily out of work. Few of them had alternatives. This client demography is one reason outdoor relief proved so resilient, as statistics of its distribution, problematic as they are, clearly reveal. The prevalence of outdoor relief varied more with state policy than with economic conditions, although everywhere outside the South it remained important. For example, in Connecticut, the number receiving outdoor relief varied from about 4 per 1,000 population in 1880 and 1890 to around 5 in both 1900 and 1910.[16] In neighboring Massachusetts, the numbers were much larger: approximately 20 in 1890; 24 in 1900; and 17 in 1910. By contrast, in Virginia in 1910, the number was about 2.5, while in New Hampshire it exceeded 25 in the same year. Similar differences characterized the proportion of the population aided by indoor relief in various states. Clearly, more people received outdoor than indoor relief. In Connecticut, the number receiving indoor relief varied from roughly 2,000 and 5,000 per year between 1898 and the late 1920s; the number receiving outdoor relief varied much more, for instance, from just under 15,000 in 1898 to about 40,000 in 1919 and just over 30,000 in 1927. Similarly, in Massachusetts between 1889 and 1929, the number receiving indoor relief remained flat, around 10,000 to 15,000 each year, while the number receiving outdoor relief was both more variable and much larger, around 70,000 at the turn of the century and just under 140,000 in 1928.

Nonetheless, indoor relief remained more expensive than outdoor, both on a per capita basis and as a total expenditure. In Connecticut, per capita spending on outdoor relief, except for 1916–17, varied from approximately $20 to $30 between 1898 and 1927; per capita spending

---

and Political Culture in San Francisco, 1860–1906 (Berkeley and Los Angeles: University of California Press, 1986); and Robin L. Einhorn, *Property Rules: Political Economy in Chicago, 1833–1872* (Chicago: University of Chicago Press, 1991).

[16] These figures were compiled by Tim Hacsi. I appreciate his excellent work. The sources of the figures are listed in the appendix to my essay "The Mixed Economy of Social Welfare in the United States," in Michael B. Katz and Christoph Sachsse, eds., *The Mixed Economy of Social Welfare: Public/Private Relations in England, Germany, and the United States from the 1870s to the 1930s* (forthcoming), which also shows the data in graphic form.

on indoor relief, much more variable, was about $90 in 1898; $160 in 1920; and $100 in 1927. As a consequence, total spending on both kinds of relief remained generally similar until 1918, when expenses for indoor relief began to soar above those for outdoor relief. By 1927, the state spent about $600,000 on outdoor and $1,200,000 on indoor relief. In Indiana, to take another example, from 1900 to 1925 spending on indoor relief always outstripped that on outdoor relief by substantial margins. Within states, interestingly, it appears that smaller, rural communities often spent more generously on relief than did larger ones.

Despite the continued importance of relief, voluntarism remained a ubiquitous feature of America's response to dependence. Its many strands encompassed a variety of methods, agencies, religious impulses, and exposed the tense, complicated relations among gender, ethnicity, and class. Two points about this complex history are particularly important here. First, voluntarism reflected long-standing assumptions about the responsibility of elites for supervising the behavior of the poor. From the early decades of the nineteenth century through its close, reformers periodically lamented that neglect by their betters permitted the spread of immorality among the urban poor, who, they said, lived increasingly isolated lives. (The argument has echoes in current dismay about the alleged withdrawal of the black middle class from inner cities and the consequent social isolation of the residents that remain.) The answer, they argued, was the reassertion of social control through deference and personal relations embodied in a distinctive strategy: friendly visiting. First advocated by Robert Hartley and the Association for Improving the Condition of the Poor in the 1840s, friendly visiting became the cornerstone of the charity organization movement later in the century. Similar assumptions about the role of elites stimulated both the formation of the New York State Charities Aid Society in 1873, which successfully won legislation permitting it to investigate local poorhouses, and the delegation of police powers to the private Societies for the Prevention of Cruelty to Children (SPCC), first founded in the late 1870s. Indeed, the delegation to voluntary associations of the power to investigate and coerce points to a second key feature of America's response to dependence:

37

its mixed public/private economy. Throughout American history, governments often have met their public goals through the delegation of responsibility and funds to nominally private agencies. The result has been a bewildering mixture of practices not usefully classified as either public or private.

For example, in New York State in 1897, the income of charitable institutions was about $21,293,732. Of this amount, the state contributed $1.5 million; the counties, $2.5 million; and cities $5.5 million. Fees for inmate support supplied $1.25 million; donations and voluntary contributions, $2.5 million; membership fees, $1.5 million; legacies, $750,000; investment interest, $1 million; entertainments, $400,000; sales of bonds, stocks, and other investments, $1 million; loans, $1.5 million; and all other sources, $2.5 million. On October 1, 1897, 66,585 inmates, or about 1 percent of the state's population, lived in these institutions, and hundreds of thousands of others received aid in their own homes.[17] Not only was the economy of relief mixed; it was, even in the late-nineteenth century, a big business.

Nineteenth-century voluntarism crystallized in the Scientific Charity Movement embodied in the Charity Organization Societies, imported from Great Britain first in Buffalo, New York, in 1878. Scientific charity inherited a method (friendly visiting); a key operational distinction (the difference between the worthy and unworthy poor); and an enemy (outdoor relief). At the same time, its incorporation of social Darwinist views of social evolution, its centralized organizational model, and its fear of class war marked it as unmistakably modern for its time. Its hostility to conventional relief practices rested partly on ideology and partly on its sponsors' belief in the inescapable incompetence and corruption of government. The essential features of charity organization were: centralized citywide registers of all relief recipients, maintained by a special agency; the investigation of applicants for relief for other agencies; the replacement of public outdoor relief with private assistance; the supervision of the poor through friendly visiting; and the collection of data on pauperism, relief, and related

---

[17] "State Inspection of Charities," newspaper clipping, source unknown, "SPCC—Clippings" folder, box 161, Community Service Society collection, Rare Books and Manuscripts Room, Butler Library, Columbia University.

subjects. Everywhere, the form of Charity Organization Societies reflected local circumstances, and none of them exactly matched the ideal model. In part, the problem reflected rivalries among local agencies, religious antagonisms, and the resilience of patronage politics; it also highlighted the impossibility of reducing class estrangement, isolation, and dependence in large industrial cities by reasserting class control through deference and face-to-face relations. Even more, the Charity Organization Societies' model and methods proved incapable of coping with the misery in late-nineteenth- and early-twentieth-century American cities. Indeed, a cataclysmic event, the depression of the 1890s, revealed the bankruptcy of existing relief practices, leaving Charity Organization Societies often reactionary rather than progressive forces in the shaping of social policy, sometimes internally divided between reforming administrators and supporters of entrenched practices that persisted relatively unchanged into the early decades of the new century.

One other relief strategy of the Poorhouse Era deserves special mention: the separation of parents and children. Distrust of poor parents' competence combined with fears of social disorder to override the sentimental exaltation of domesticity that shaped writing about home and family. Observers repeatedly commented on the negligence and immorality of city parents whose fondness for drink, reluctance to work, and inability to teach middle-class behavior left their children wild, ignorant, and unprepared for work, potential criminals and paupers. As a response, reformers devised various ways of intervening between parents and children. First among them was schools, initially Sunday schools sponsored by Protestant denominations, shortly afterward free primary schools for the children of the poor, and a little later public school systems. For the especially recalcitrant, states founded reformatories, and legislation transferred custody of their inmates from parents to the state. (In their early years, parents initiated most committals of children to reformatories, which they viewed as temporary refuges for times of crises or ways of disciplining uncontrollable children; they often did not realize that they were surrendering not only their children's care but their custody as well.) In the 1850s, Charles Loring Brace introduced the most dramatic strategy for separating parents and children. His New York Children's Aid Society shipped city children to the West to live with farm families. From 1853 to the mid-1890s, the Children's Aid Society moved at least ninety thousand children out of New York City. Even an apparently humane reform in the second half of the nineteenth century, the removal of children from poorhouses, contributed to family breakup, for it forced parents unable to support themselves through work or outdoor relief to send their children to orphanages. Without doubt, children suffered horribly in poorhouses, but alternatives did exist, notably the support of families in their own homes. The alternative chosen, therefore, underlines the importance of family breakup as one goal of public policy.

Public officials and reformers nonetheless faced a delicate question: how to force a family to surrender its children. Who would identify families that abused or neglected their children? Who would initiate their prosecution? Reformers answered by founding Societies for the Prevention of Cruelty to Children (SPCC), first in New York City in 1876. Known as the "Gerry" Societies, after their principal founder, Elderbridge Gerry, or, to the poor, as "the Cruelty," SPCCs were voluntary agencies vested with quasi-police powers. They encouraged neighbors to spy on one another, investigated cases referred to them by other agencies, initiated prosecutions, and, at least in New York, incarcerated children awaiting trial. In Philadelphia, when the SPCC asked courts to remove children from their families, they also requested jail terms for their parents to prevent them from interfering with their children's placement. In New York, the Charity Organization Society often tried to force parents to send their children to school or improve their care by threatening to report them to the SPCC.

Throughout the Poorhouse Era, relief's complex public/private economy reflected a debate about the appropriate institutional models for public policy. I call the four major models paternalistic voluntarism, corporate voluntarism, democratic localism, and bureaucracy. Conflict among them marked not only the history of relief but of education and other areas of social policy as well. Paternalistic voluntarism reflected noblesse oblige. It rested on faith in the talented amateur and, at an administrative level, scorned the need for state control or professional staff. It was also a class system of education or philanthropy, a means for one class to civilize another and thereby ensure that society would remain tolerable, orderly, and safe. Democratic localists sought to adapt to the city organizational forms current in rural areas: small in scale, community controlled. They rested their case on faith in people and hostility to imposed social change. Corporate voluntarism was the conduct of single institutions as individual corporations operated by self-perpetuating boards of trustees and financed either wholly through endowment or through a combination of endowment and fees, sometimes with help from government. To its sponsors, corporate voluntarism appeared to combine the virtues of the other two models. Without the stigma of lower-class affiliation, it offered disinterested, enlightened, and continuous management that kept the operation of institutions out of the rough and unpredictable play of politics. At the same time, by placing each institution under a different administrative authority, it retained the limited scope essential to variety, flexibility, and adaptation to local circumstance. Moreover, this corporate mode of control matched arrangements for managing both other forms of public business and private enterprise. Incipient bureaucrats, by contrast, stressed centralization, efficiency, system, and the importance of both public finance and control. Committed to the importance of expertise and supervision, they led campaigns to professionalize their specialties.

In the history of relief, the major voluntary agencies reflected paternalistic voluntarism. The variety of individually chartered institutions governed by their own boards of trustees exemplified corporate voluntarism, even in the public sector. The first major examples of bureaucracy were State Boards of Charities (similar agencies often had different names), initially created in the late 1860s to rationalize relief practices; an example from the 1890s is New York state's contentious and partial replacement of county mental hospitals by a system of large state institutions. Resistance to the abolition of local institutions and outdoor relief showed the persistence throughout the century of the values underlying democratic localism.

The competition among institutional models refocuses the discussion about relations between public and private in the history of

American welfare practice, for the source of authority and finance formed only two topics in debates about institutional structure, control, and administration. Interestingly, in relief, bureaucratic models failed to triumph as completely as they did in public education. American state and local governments never developed any organizational structure for relief remotely comparable to public educational systems. Nor did professional certification develop the lock on social work that it did on teaching. Instead, corporate forms remained far more widespread in both private and public sectors, with public money financing many nominally private institutions. This reliance on corporate models reflected a variety of influences: an American preference for voluntarism, the increasing domination of corporations in economic organization, the underdevelopment of public administration, a distrust of patronage politics, and, as Ellis Hawley argues, a weak administrative sector that "sought to enhance its capacity by bringing private administrative resources into 'public service.'"[18]

THE CONSTRUCTION OF THE SEMIWELFARE STATE

Reluctant or not, American reformers from the 1890s to the 1930s did help build a series of bureaucracies that formed the skeleton of America's semiwelfare state. In the process, they attempted to discard some of the key strategies of the Poorhouse Era. Child saving first revealed these changes. Contemporaries used *child saving* as a generic term to describe a variety of efforts to improve the lives of children. As a movement, it became a magnet drawing together a diverse but effective coalition active from roughly the 1890s to World War I. Its major components were these: the removal of children from almshouses; the replacement of institutions with foster care; the introduction of juvenile courts and probation; educational reform through compulsory education, day care, kindergartens, and playgrounds; the attempted abolition of child labor; advocacy of mothers' pensions; and support for public health measures to reduce infant mortality, curb tuberculosis, and modify the delivery of health care.

[18] Hawley, "Social Policy and the Liberal State," p. 127.

Three debates permeated the child-saving movement. The first concerned the relative merits of institutions and families as settings for dependent children. The second reconsidered the strategy of family breakup; and the third questioned the appropriate role for government in the administration and provision of services and relief. Of these, the role of government proved the most contentious question, often pitting eastern reformers, revolted by corruption and patronage politics, against those from the Midwest, who favored a far more extensive role for public authorities. (Midwestern reformers did not confront the entrenched voluntary establishment so influential in the East.) By 1909, the first White House Conference on Children revealed a rough consensus on the issues. Institutions, almost all commentators now argued, harmed children, who should be placed whenever possible in foster homes; despite the continued importance of voluntary agencies, the responsibilities and supervisory authority of government should be extended, even to the relations between parents and children; and whenever possible, both public and private action should try to preserve rather than to break up families. All these recommendations, it should be stressed, aimed to reform practice in state and local governments and private agencies; no one yet expected the federal government to become a major player in the administration or direction of aid to dependent children.

Child saving emerged from a variety of sources: new ideas about childhood, anxieties generated by mounting divorce and falling white-native birthrates, the professionalization of reform and faith in experts, and theories that stressed the benevolence of the state and the possibility of reconciling diverse interests without class conflict. As a movement, it culminated with the introduction of mothers' pensions. Mothers' pensions embodied the new commitment to family preservation, which required a stipend large enough to allow widows to support their children without full-time work. Advocates of mothers' pensions included western and midwestern juvenile court judges, many settlement workers, women leading Jewish charity organizations in New York City, representatives of women's organizations, public welfare officials, progressive representatives of private charity, and, after 1912, the United States Children's Bureau. Opposition came primarily from eastern representatives of private charity, notably from the large Charity Organization Societies. In 1911, Missouri and Illinois became the first states to introduce mothers' pensions; by the end of 1913, twenty others, primarily western and central, had followed. By 1919, mothers' pensions existed in thirty-nine states and the territories of Alaska and Hawaii.

In 1931, these programs supported 200,000 children in every state except Georgia and South Carolina. To be sure, they were small, paid almost exclusively to widows, reached only a fraction of eligible recipients, and demanded long residence, sometimes proof of citizenship, and almost always good behavior. Nonetheless, they prevented the breakup of many families and represented an important, if halting, step on the road from charity to entitlement. Indeed, they became the precedent for the Aid to Dependent Children provisions of the 1935 Economic Security Act, which, of course, later became Aid to Families with Dependent Children, or what Americans customarily call "welfare." Mothers' pensions also helped legitimate government supervision of families because state governments needed to ensure adequate treatment for the children of the families they helped preserve. Family preservation, therefore, sanctioned rather than challenged governments' intrusion into the relations between parents and children.

In the late-nineteenth and early-twentieth centuries, reformers expanded government's role to embrace broader interests, redesigned its structure to rely more on administration by experts, and increased its regulation of both commercial and noncommercial private activity. As state governments took on new tasks, they began to reorganize and professionalize their administrations. New York's 1929 Public Welfare Law signaled the new spirit. Relief became public welfare; almshouses became county, city, or town homes; superintendents of the poor, county commissioners of public welfare; overseers of the poor, public welfare officers; the State Board of Charities, the State Board of Social Welfare.[19] In short, welfare participated in the transformation of nineteenth-century America's "government of courts and

---

[19] Joan M. Crouse, *The Homeless Transient in the Great Depression, 1929–1941* (Albany: State University of New York Press, 1986), pp. 24, 41.

parties" into its twentieth-century government of bureaucracies and regulatory agencies with expanded social tasks, new divisions among levels of government, and a shift in the institutions making and implementing policy. The nineteenth century's party system with its high voter turnout gave way, Richard L. McCormick emphasizes, to a new pattern in which far fewer people voted, parties were less important, and governance relied increasingly on agencies of regulation and administration.[20]

In this reorganization of government, municipal reform held special implications for relief and welfare. The explosive expansion, diversification, and industrialization of late-nineteenth-century American cities overwhelmed existing city governments, which often were little more than confederations of wards run by party machines. As a consequence, cities—despite some remarkable achievements—as a whole lacked the capacity to respond decisively and with coordination to everyday problems, like the need for sewers, water, electric lights, street paving, and better transportation, or to confront overcrowded housing, high rates of disease and mortality, poor schools, and endemic poverty. Like reformers confronting nineteenth-century business practices, municipal reformers looked for ways to manage structures that had outgrown their means of administration. To a considerable degree, municipal reforms succeeded in expanding and rationalizing city governments. One measure is the rise in per capita spending by the nation's largest cities: 3 percent from 1904 to 1912 and 59 percent from 1912 to 1930. In the first of these two periods, spending on charity declined by 8 percent, and in the second, it leaped by 79 percent.

The municipal reform movement tried to recast urban governance. Its goals for large cities were increased autonomy from state legislatures; a strong role for the mayor, who would have the power to appoint top officials and veto budget items; a smaller, unicameral legislature elected at large; and bureaus reorganized into series of spe-

[20] The phrase "government of courts and parties" is from Stephen Skowronek, *Building a New American State: The Expansion of National Administrative Capacities* (New York: Cambridge University Press, 1982); the reorganization of government in the early-twentieth century is a theme in McCormick, *The Party Period*.

cialized departments run by experts. For smaller cities, reformers recommended commissions and city managers.

Starting with Kansas City in 1913, many cities created municipal welfare departments to administer their growing relief budgets and municipal research bureaus to gather data on their problems. (Southern cities by and large did not create municipal welfare departments until the 1930s.)[21] Both reflected the goals common to municipal reform: centralization, efficiency, and science. They were also a strategy for dampening the growing radicalism that frightened local business interests. In 1916, city welfare departments primarily from the Midwest and West formed the National Public Welfare League; eastern cities joined them by and large only as the resistance of private charity interests weakened after World War I. Objections to outdoor relief also had eroded by the eve of World War I. In the 1870s and 1880s most municipal reformers as well as charity workers had condemned outdoor relief; by about 1915 most accepted it, if grudgingly, for they had learned to appreciate the magnitude and intractability of urban poverty and, as professionals, argued that the source of funds mattered less than their administration. As a consequence, they transformed outdoor relief from a question of principle into one of management.

Through the creation of financial federations or Community Chests (pioneered in Cleveland in 1914), modern management also transformed voluntarism. Appreciated especially by businessmen as sources of economy and control, Community Chests grew slowly until World War I, when their numbers exploded from 12 in 1919 to 329 in 1929. Despite their rhetorical commitment to inclusion, Community Chests reinforced the forces of convention and social order. They excluded many reform, radical, and labor organizations and did not, by and large, fund culture. Instead, they helped engineer the transformation of charity into philanthropy and to broaden the base of giving outward from the very wealthy to a much larger section of the social structure. They also escalated the bureaucratization of private charity and hastened the redefinition of volunteers from friendly visitors to

[21] Douglas L. Smith, *The New Deal in the Urban South* (Baton Rouge: Louisiana State University Press, 1988), pp. 46–164.

fund-raisers, in the process hardening the distinction between volunteers and professionals.

Because they entered the new industrial era with outdated labor and management practices, businesses faced problems analogous to cities. Vast operations strung out through several sites frustrated coordination and informal hiring practices; by fostering high labor turnover, they created irregular employment and defeated attempts to build a stable, loyal workforce. Confronted with these problems, management deployed various strategies. One was repression: crushing labor unrest. Another was wresting control of the manufacturing process away from skilled workers and foremen. A third attempted to clear the labor market of unproductive workers through immigration restriction, child labor laws, enforced retirement, compulsory education, and eugenics. A fourth was called welfare capitalism.

Welfare capitalism embraced a variety of innovative practices. In fact, corporations proved more daring than public officials and pioneered social insurance practices later adopted by governments. The first examples of welfare capitalism, industrial villages like Pullman, Illinois, founded in the late-nineteenth century, soon proved a dead end for labor policy. Indeed, only after 1900 did welfare capitalism, promoted by several regional and national organizations, emerge as a national movement. In 1904, the National Civic Federation created a Welfare Department, and some universities began to offer courses in industrial welfare around the same time. With businesses eager to increase production, prevent disruptive labor disputes, and deflect the potential influence of Bolshevism, corporate adoption of welfare policies accelerated by World War I. Welfare capitalist schemes included savings and home-ownership plans, stock purchasing, insurance and pensions designed to protect workers and their families from accident, illness, old age, and death; improved plant conditions, safety, and medical services; and the introduction of visiting nurses, sports, educational and cultural programs, and personal counseling. Again, new practices crystallized into a novel profession: personnel manager. Formed in 1918, the National Association of Personnel Managers attracted two thousand to its 1919 convention and more than five thousand in 1920.

47

Although many aspects of welfare capitalism became more or less standard features of personnel practice, they failed to win the undivided loyalty of workers, check the growth of a labor movement, or ensure workers adequate, steady wages and safe, humane working conditions. Indeed, the Great Depression of the 1930s underlined the fragility of welfare capitalism as a source of protection for working people and their families. By the post–World War II era, both labor and capital spoke of fringe benefits rather than welfare capitalism. Lacking adequate public social insurance, labor adopted these innovations pioneered by capital as bargaining chips in the construction of a private welfare state.

State governments hesitantly introduced new forms of social insurance during the same years corporations pioneered private welfare practice. First came workmen's compensation. From 1909 to 1920, forty-three states passed workmen's compensation legislation, which responded not only to the recommendations of academic experts but to the needs of labor, businesses, and insurance companies as well. Increasingly, workers injured at an extraordinarily high rate in American industries successfully sued employers for damages. However, although workers might win, court cases could drag on for years before the injured received any benefits. At the same time, employers and insurance companies found the situation unpredictable and expensive, and academic reformers objected to existing practices because they did not encourage industry to prevent accidents. Responding to these problems, early workmen's compensation laws generally favored business interests. They prohibited injured workers from suing, remained voluntary rather than compulsory, and relied on private insurance companies instead of state governments. At first, courts administered many of them, but the results proved disastrous, and, as the nation moved away from a government of courts and parties, the administration of workmen's compensation passed to new industrial commissions. Rates of compensation remained very low, rarely more than ten dollars per week, and usually lasted no longer than three hundred or four hundred weeks for total disability or death. In short, despite the new legislation, disabled workers and their families still suffered severe loss of income and security.

Unemployment and old-age insurance developed much more slowly than did workmen's compensation. Only in 1932 did Wisconsin become the first state to pass an unemployment compensation bill. Early-twentieth-century economists approached unemployment cautiously because of their reluctance to interfere with markets. Instead of insurance, they advocated labor exchanges and other measures intended to stabilize labor demand. None of these worked. Although a few private corporations introduced their own unemployment funds, these vanished in hard times, and union schemes proved no more durable. Fearing that pooled state insurance funds would degenerate into a demoralizing dole, as they alleged had happened in Great Britain and Germany, Wisconsin labor experts advocated plans based on segregated reserve funds with distinct accounts for every employer and bonuses for those providing steady employment. Other social insurance advocates, led by an Ohio-based group, argued that only pooled funds would prove large and flexible enough to meet all contingencies. For them, relief was more important than prevention. Resisted by business interests and, until the Great Depression, even by some labor spokesmen, unemployment insurance remained contentious. As a result, by 1935 only five states had passed unemployment legislation.

From 1867 to 1912, the federal government operated a massive social insurance scheme for the elderly: veterans' pensions. In 1912, the $153 million spent on them amounted to 18 percent of the federal budget. As expenses for veterans' pensions ebbed with the death of the Civil War generation, support for public pensions for the elderly mounted. The forced retirement of older workers in industries and civil service jobs, the growing proportion of the population over the age of sixty, and a revolt against the incarceration of the elderly in institutions all fed the demand for government action to support the aged. Late in the nineteenth century, a few firms had introduced their own limited pension plans; these increased after 1910 with industry's new attempts to reduce labor turnover. However, they spread most quickly and broadly in the public sector. From 1911 to 1935, thirty-three state legislatures introduced compulsory retirement and pensions for teachers. By the late 1920s, retirement funds for policemen, firemen, and teachers had become nearly universal. In 1911, Massachusetts became the first state to pass a pension law covering all employees. As of 1931, pension laws had passed in twelve states, but pension funds were mandatory in only three (New York, California, and Wyoming). Even when states or counties did introduce pensions, the amounts paid were tiny and reached a very small number of people. Nonetheless, because the elderly formed a powerful cross-class coalition, they succeeded in mounting a major national movement, which placed their concerns at the top of the New Deal's social agenda.

The early social insurance movement underscored the limits of voluntarism and the necessity of national legislation. Clearly, neither businesses nor unions could insure the welfare of their employees or members; strategies based on prevention neglected crucial needs for relief; by themselves, administrative centralization and efficiency could not overcome the deficiencies of inadequate policies and funds; and government's customary reluctance to extend public authority into economic relations had allowed economic insecurity and hardship to flourish. Finally, the Great Depression proved that state and local governments lacked both the administrative and fiscal capacity to meet the legitimate needs of their citizens.

The Great Depression followed a decade of significant state expansion of funding for welfare-related activities and administrative reform. From 1920 to 1931, state and local spending (in millions of dollars) rose for education from $1,705 to $2,311; highways, $1,294 to $1,742; hospitals, $200 to $349; and public welfare, $119 to $444. Like New York, other states changed the names of their State Boards of Charities (or related agencies) to Departments of Public (or Social) Welfare, and their superintendents of the poor became commissioners of public welfare. Although not universal, these common changes accompanied the increasing centralization of welfare administration. By 1930, twenty-six states had created single departments of public welfare; in seventeen states two or more departments shared major statewide welfare functions. From 1917 to 1930, the states introduced at least forty-four new agencies with statewide responsibilities.[22]

[22] William R. Brock, *Welfare, Democracy, and the New Deal* (New York: Cambridge University Press), pp. 2–23.

Nonetheless, the new social work schools enrolled only 2,000 students in 1930, and but 10 percent of these completed their course. Only 8 percent of the country's 6,809 hospitals (and half of these were in New York and Massachusetts) had social service departments. Nor had school social work become universal: thirty-four states employed 275 visiting teachers. Similarly, half the country's factories had personnel departments. Of the country's 31,241 social workers, 24,592 were women, whose average pay was less than that of an elementary schoolteacher. In the states, a bewildering variety of local authorities still administered relief. In Massachusetts, each of 355 towns and counties had distinct units for poor relief. In Pennsylvania, approximately 535 laws still governed poor relief in 1934; in 676 counties, 967 people legally administered poor relief in 425 districts, 366 of which crowded into 15 counties. In New Hampshire, 700 different officials administered public relief in 245 separate county, city, and town units, of which 140 had fewer than 1,000 people and 14 more than 5,000. In Ohio in 1934, 1,535 local government units retained some responsibility for poor relief.

For various reasons the Great Depression was an unprecedented economic disaster: the scale of the collapse, the magnitude of unemployment, its reach into the ranks of salaried and professional workers, and the absence of customary cyclical recovery. All these imposed demands on local governments that exhausted their financial resources for relief and left them clamoring for help. People had used up their own savings; those of friends, relatives, and private agencies were overwhelmed; and the reserves of unions and individual firms had collapsed. At the same time, militant organizations clamored for change: unemployed workers' councils on the political Left; Huey Long's supporters; the Townsend Movement among the elderly. Clearly, the circumstances demanded action by the federal government. The question was what form it should take. President Herbert Hoover's initial attempts to secure voluntary compliance from business and to stimulate spending through loans soon proved ineffective. It was left to President Franklin Roosevelt and his administration to find a more direct approach.

The new administration put the federal government directly into the business of relief, or public assistance, for the first time. On May 12, 1933, Congress authorized the creation of the Federal Emergency Relief Administration (FERA) modeled after a similar agency, the TERA, founded by Franklin Roosevelt when he was governor of New York. Harry Hopkins, former director of the Temporary Emergency Relief Association and, before that, first director of New York's Board of Child Welfare, which administered mothers' pensions, headed the new federal relief effort funded through a combination of matching and discretionary grants. From May 1933 to its termination on June 30, 1936, the FERA spent over $3 billion. With benefits that varied from state to state, it supported both direct and work relief. The FERA also sponsored Federal Transient Camps, the first federal response to the problem of the homeless unemployed and an attempt to circumvent local settlement laws, which still plagued relief.[23] Also in 1933, another new agency, the Federal Surplus Relief Corporation, began to distribute surplus commodities.[24] The FERA not only moved federal funds to the needy; its matching grants forced states to increase their spending, and the conditions attached to its grants forced them to improve their administrative practices. The FERA also stimulated the development of the public welfare sector because it granted money only to public agencies. Nonetheless, the FERA and the New Deal vastly increased the influence on government of private social workers because it hired them in large numbers to plan and administer its new programs. Along with other New Deal agencies, the FERA had another significance: it helped change the nature of American federalism. The Constitution allocated government functions by level; generally, state and federal governments had distinct responsibilities. New Deal programs did not usurp state functions. Instead, they influenced them through the conditions attached to grants offered states for activities by and large never before funded by the federal government. As a result, American federalism increasingly became a system of shared rather than parallel responsibilities, and matching grants became the preferred mechanism for influencing state action.

[23] The story of the transient camps is told well in Crouse, *Homeless Transient*.

[24] For federal agricultural relief policies, see the excellent discussion in Janet Poppendieck, *Breadlines Knee-Deep in Wheat: Food Assistance in the Great Depression* (New Brunswick, N.J.: Rutgers University Press), 1986.

The federal government tried to alleviate the unemployment crisis among young people through special programs, notably the Civilian Conservation Corps (authorized March 1933), which, at its peak in August 1935, employed 505,000 young men in 2,600 camps. The National Youth Administration (1936) aided primarily high school age students with work. Before it closed in 1941 (the same year the CCC ended), it aided about 400,000 students. Nonetheless, the early New Deal's major work program was the Civil Works Administration (CWA), created to supplement the FERA's work relief and reduce the suffering and disorder predicted for the winter of 1933–34. Authorized in November 1933, by January 1934 the CWA employed 4 million people at public works jobs administered directly by the federal government. Unlike the FERA, it paid wages negotiated by the Public Works Administration, which were higher than those based on relief standards. The greatest public works experiment in American history, the CWA at its peak employed 4.26 million workers representing about 8 million households, or 22.2 percent of the American population. Within the CWA, management and efficiency experts edged social workers from power by consciously abandoning casework and rejecting means tests. Thus, when fiscal conservatives, business interests, and southern Democrats attacked the CWA, social workers proved notably absent among its defenders.

President Roosevelt, who disliked relief, thought of federal involvement as only a temporary response to an emergency. By removing the federal government from public assistance, he accentuated a distinction between public assistance and social insurance, which became a cornerstone of the America's semiwelfare state. Early in his administration, he decided to find a more permanent policy. Believing the federal government should assume responsibility for "employable" workers and turn relief of the others back to the states, he ordered the replacement of the FERA and CWA with a federal work program, the Works Progress Administration, intended as a temporary response to a national emergency, and the establishment of a system of income security or social insurance. Despite the administration's assurances, widespread suffering followed the abolition of the FERA in 1935 and the transfer of the Federal Surplus Relief Corporation to the Department of Agriculture, which transposed a program designed to feed needy people into one intended to aid large farmers through raising prices and helping them dispose of unmarketable products.[25] (The Agricultural Adjustment Act also aided large southern farmers at the expense of their often black tenants, who found themselves without land, jobs, or income.) The WPA differed from the CWA. First, it was decentralized. State and local agencies planned and sponsored programs, with the exception of its arts program and a few others. It also increased the role of social workers, who investigated all applicants for relief. In sharp contrast to the CWA, the WPA employed but one member from any family, and it pegged its wages between relief payments and pay offered by the private sector, at what it called "security wages." Many families eligible for work under the CWA proved ineligible under the WPA, which, despite its massive size, helped only about one-fourth of the eligible unemployed.

With mounting pressure from a variety of sources and a mandate from the congressional elections of 1934, President Roosevelt initiated planning for a national system of social insurance by appointing the Committee on Economic Security, chaired by Edwin Witte, an academic from Wisconsin. Guided by the principles of the Wisconsin approach to social insurance, the CES recommended an extensive system including national health insurance and public works. (Both proved too controversial for the administration to accept.) Nonetheless, the CES's recommendations were far from radical. Indeed, they rested on what Jerry Cates calls the "conservative social insurance ideology": risk selection, or the targeting of carefully chosen constituencies, the contribution of workers to their own insurance, and the payment of unequal benefits reflecting prior wages.

Despite these principles, the legislation that resulted, the Economic Security Act of 1935, introduced a few key noncontributory programs. Most important were federal old-age pensions, a matching grant program to assist the elderly who had not worked long enough to collect benefits under the new social insurance program, and Aid to Dependent Children, slipped into the act by the Children's Bureau as an inexpensive way to help widows with families. ADC, ironically, became the largest public assistance program, synonymous, eventually, with

[25] Poppendieck, *Breadlines*, pp. 224–25, 249.

what we inaccurately call welfare. The Economic Security Act also extended federal aid to the blind, increased appropriations for the Public Health Service, and supported vocational rehabilitation and infant and maternal health programs. Most immediately important and controversial, however, were contributory programs: unemployment insurance and Social Security for the elderly. Social Security emerged as a fully federally run program excluding agricultural and domestic workers—hence most African Americans—and paying low initial benefits. Unemployment insurance was a combined federal-state program funded partly by employee contributions.

The New Deal's immediate legacy to the working class came neither through public assistance nor social insurance. It resulted instead from labor legislation. With section 7A of the 1933 National Recovery Act, the federal government began to support labor's right to organize. In 1935, the Wagner Act (sustained by the Supreme Court in 1937) created a National Labor Relations Board, authorized to conduct collective bargaining elections and regulate labor practices. The Fair Labor Standards Act protected labor with a minimum wage, a maximum workweek, and the prohibition of child labor, though its provisions still excluded the most exploitive categories of work. This new support helped revive the labor movement, which had been devastated by a business offensive in the 1920s. It also facilitated the formation and spectacular growth of the Congress of Industrial Organizations, which organized unskilled and semiskilled industrial workers and challenged the craft-based American Federation of Labor. Because unions used collective bargaining to win health care and other benefits not provided by Congress, the Wagner Act and other labor legislation chartered the growth of a private welfare state.

Nonetheless, the New Deal irrevocably tipped the balance between public and private in favor of the former. As William Brock points out, it "brought public agencies to the center of the stage and relegated private charities to the wings."[26] Indeed, government spending for social welfare increased massively. For all levels of government, spending from 1932 to 1939 leaped from $208 million to $4.9 billion. In both 1913 and 1923 public aid accounted for 1 percent of government

[26] Brock, *Welfare*, p. 358.

expenses; in 1933, 6.5 percent; and in 1939, 27.1 percent. Per capita spending for public aid rose from $0.57 in 1923 to $37.80 in 1939. At the same time, New Deal matching grant legislation forced states to expand their commitment to social welfare. In 1935, eight states had passed unemployment insurance laws; two years later they were universal. The Economic Security Act also forced states to improve the quality of their administration and professionalize their staffs. Still, the expansion of the federal social role greatly reduced the proportion of welfare expenses borne by state and local governments. That is, although state and local expenses rose from $203 million to $1.9 billion from 1932 to 1939, their share of the total decreased from 97.9 percent to 37.5 percent.

Despite its innovations, the New Deal cemented into American welfare policy a distinction between social insurance and public assistance that has blocked the creation of a comprehensive program of economic security to protect all citizens. (Chapter 2 discusses some of the subsequent attempts to respond to poverty by extending or cutting back social welfare.) Many writers of every political persuasion have documented the inadequacy of America's welfare state. Theorists have offered several reasons for its stunted development. Recent critics have pointed to the distinction between public assistance and social insurance as a major obstacle preventing its expansion. Few accounts, however, have strayed beyond social insurance to emphasize the persistence of outdoor relief throughout modern American history. Nonetheless, outdoor relief remains a massive, unsettled issue, although now discussed in the updated vocabulary of welfare. Indeed, in recent years, local, state, and federal governments have used cutbacks in General Assistance, AFDC, and other programs to launch another of America's periodic wars on outdoor relief, or welfare.

Because they have emphasized social insurance and paid more attention to the rhetoric of reform than to the relief of dependency, historians have underestimated the scope and role of relief during the last two hundred years. Instead, by often taking voluntary agencies at their own word, historians have overemphasized their importance. Historians, usually unintentionally, have reinforced the myth of voluntarism's potential for solving America's social problems and reified the blurred and shifting boundaries between public and private. In truth, both public and private remain protean, socially constructed, historically contingent concepts, never fixed categories. In social welfare, education, criminal justice, municipal administration, and economic development, the enduring contest over their meaning has escalated into one of the key policy debates of our time.

The hegemony of market models also has constrained constructive debate about welfare and poverty. By accepting the separation of economics and politics embedded in nineteenth-century liberal thought, discourse on poverty and welfare reifies the market as the regulator of economic relations. Intrusion in the market or interference with its natural workings becomes, by definition, illegitimate and destructive. Government policy that redistributes or supports income is redefined as contrary to the laws of nature. At the same time, market models answer one of the enduring questions about welfare—What, as a society, do we owe each other?—in terms of exchange. The measure of success is concrete returns for dollars invested in welfare. With only a few exceptions (notably, in recent years, the pastoral letter on the economy written by Catholic bishops), both conservative and liberal welfare analysts use as their criteria for evaluating or justifying welfare wage rates, productivity, and economic efficiency. One example is the obsession of liberal economists during the Great Society era with the impact of income supports on work incentives. With the partial exception of legal scholars and moral philosophers, no recent American students of poverty and welfare have advanced the theoretical foundations of the welfare state or transcended the conventional boundaries of a liberalism that almost everyone agrees has grown stale.[27] Together liberals and conservatives produced a welfare literature bounded by a narrow and constricted vision of social bonds and obligations that eased the way for the conservative revival in the 1980s.

---

[27] National Conference of Catholic Bishops, *Economic Justice for All: Pastoral Letter on Catholic Social Teaching and the U.S. Economy* (Washington, D.C.: United States Catholic Conference, 1986); Robert E. Goodin, *Protecting the Vulnerable: A Reanalysis of Our Social Responsibilities* (Chicago: University of Chicago Press, 1975); Michael Sherraden, *Assets and the Poor: A New American Welfare Policy* (Armonk, N.Y.: M. E. Sharpe, 1991).

In what other ways might one answer the question about the results of welfare? Instead of replying with estimates of welfare's impact on work motivation, family structure, or the labor market, one might evaluate how successfully it has relieved deprivation or suffering. Here, historical evidence becomes crucial for showing the different ways relief and welfare have served the three major urban groups that for centuries have suffered disproportionate poverty: women family heads with children, old people, and the unemployed.

Until the last few decades, most women living alone with children were widows, and virtuous widows evoked the most consistent sympathy from public officials and private charity because nearly everyone realized that women, especially with children, lacked any legal or moral way to earn a living. Only in recent decades, as AFDC recipients have become less often widows and more often young, unmarried, and black, have women with children lost their place among the deserving poor. In most cities, female benevolent societies emerged as the earliest, or among the very first, charitable associations. In the early-twentieth century, mothers' pensions became the first state-mandated income support programs. AFDC, supplemented by food stamps, Medicaid, and sometimes subsidized housing, now support women with children, but they neither lift them out of poverty nor, with few exceptions, help them toward independence, and the real value of AFDC benefits has declined about 40 percent since 1973.

Prior to the twentieth century, the status of old people fluctuated more than sentiment about poor widows. For the first three-quarters of the nineteenth century, they too usually evoked sympathy. However, although their material circumstances had not improved in any way, hardening attitudes toward poverty and relief in the third quarter of the nineteenth century significantly lessened sympathy for the elderly. Increasingly, public and private relief officials argued that most of them had fallen into poverty because of their feckless and immoral behavior. Attitudes toward old men were especially harsh. Public officials much more readily granted outdoor relief to women, and adult children more often took in their aging mothers than their fathers. Men who found themselves poor in old age, many believed, deserved little sympathy because they either had failed to work hard enough or to save for their declining years. Only when old people capitalized on their political power did they win significant gains. Social Security in the 1930s, and its extension three decades later, reflected political and demographic realities, not a shift in status or sentiment. As a result of their power, the elderly have emerged as the major social policy winners in the last twenty years. Poverty among them has fallen by about two-thirds. Despite their continuing unmet needs, their incidence of poverty now matches the rate for the population as a whole.

Unlike women with children or old people, unemployed men aroused nearly universal sympathy only during the great depression of the 1930s. Otherwise, they have remained the pariahs among the poor. Myths of the availability of work for all able-bodied men (except for wartime, this always has been a myth) have tinged the unemployed with the aroma of laziness as, for centuries, public and private policies unsuccessfully have tried to drive them from the rolls of relief and, later, welfare. As a result, aside from unemployment insurance (which supports a decreasing proportion of those without work and offers nothing to those who have not recently been part of the regular labor force), unemployed men and nonemployed women without children, as long as they are neither elderly nor disabled, find few sources of support. State General Assistance programs, one modern euphemism for outdoor relief, remain tiny, restrictive, and inadequate. Given current levels of unemployment and housing costs, one result has been the growth in homelessness and hunger. For the homeless, local governments have reinvented poorhouses and renamed them shelters.[28]

[28] Dennis P. Culhane, "The Quandaries of Shelter Reform: An Appraisal of Efforts to 'Manage' Homelessness," *Social Service Review* (September 1992): 428–40.

The "Underclass"

In 1987, the Rockefeller Foundation asked the Social Science Research Council to consider creating a committee on the urban underclass. Robert Pearson, an SSRC staff member, asked me if I would attend a meeting of researchers to discuss the foundation's request. At the time, I was writing the War on Poverty chapter of *The Undeserving Poor*. Although I was unsure of what a historian could contribute to the contemporary discussion, the chance to learn about the latest social science research, to watch a national research agenda take shape, to learn firsthand about the working of foundations and the formulation of policy proved irresistible, although I found the word *underclass* offensive and unhelpful.

If the SSRC launched a major initiative in poverty research, I thought, it would prove, at the least, an instructive example of the distinctive triangular relations among academics, foundations, and policy in America. In the 1960s and early 1970s, these relations, I knew, had influenced the War on Poverty and the Great Society, but their inner workings remained relatively undocumented. How valuable it would be, then, to document this new round, to leave, at the minimum, a record illustrating how big social science worked in the late-twentieth century. Here was a job for a historian, and I proposed to the SSRC staff that the new committee include from the outset an archivist, who would gather and preserve documents and interview key players as the work progressed. The SSRC staff and, subsequently, the Rockefeller Foundation and the entire committee (which emerged from exploratory meetings) agreed, and I served as archivist throughout the committee's five-year history.

Listening to the debates at committee meetings, I saw the importance of history to the contemporary discussions of urban poverty, which often reflected untested historical assumptions that recent research in social history had modified or contradicted. (One example was assumptions about social relations in earlier black ghettos.) The story of contemporary urban poverty, moreover, was historical. The transformations of work, space, family, and institutions that alarmed observers and propelled major foundations to action resulted from processes embedded deep in America's past. They could not be explained apart from their origins. History was not peripheral, a quaint, diverting excursion in search of precedents and arresting parallels; it was, rather, a mode of explanation fundamental to a reconstructed social science approach to urban poverty. Still, most of the analyses of urban poverty remained impoverished because social scientists, including those on the committee, knew and thought relatively little about history. One useful way for historians to contribute to the renewed concern with urban poverty, it seemed to me, was to bring recent scholarship in social history to bear on the major issues in the debate. The committee agreed enough with my arguments to underwrite a book of historical essays, which I edited, titled *The "Underclass" Debate: Views from History*. This chapter draws on the essays gathered in the book, on my own reflections on reading them and working with the authors, and on my reservations, based on many days of attending meetings of leading social science researchers, about the directions taken by the "underclass" debate.

From 1988 through 1993, the SSRC Committee for Research on the Urban Underclass, financed largely by the Rockefeller Foundation, represented a major venture designed to reinvigorate research on urban poverty, which had languished for more than a decade, and to train a cadre of new scholars. To bring young scholars into the field, the committee developed a series of undergraduate, dissertation, and postdoctoral scholarship and fellowship programs and a predoctoral summer workshop. To encourage research, it formed a series of working groups that reviewed literature, drew up research agendas, designed research projects, and produced books. Through periodic conferences, the SSRC committee disseminated its work to wider audiences. All along, the Rockefeller Foundation had hoped that the committee would apply its research findings directly to questions of policy. Until the final days of the committee, this did not happen in any organized way. The Foundation also hoped that the committee would collaborate with the six major community action projects it funded in cities and with the policy centers whose work on poverty it partially supported. Despite several conversations among representatives of the SSRC committee, the policy centers, and the city projects, this collaboration did not take place.

In June 1992, the committee organized a by-invitation-only conference to showcase the results of its research program and to stimulate feedback for those projects in process or not yet published. At the end of the conference, a panel considered the implications of the committee's work for policy. One panel member, the director of one of the Rockefeller Foundation's six city projects, pleaded eloquently with the committee. Although the research was interesting and undoubtedly advanced knowledge about poverty, she said, it did not answer the questions that troubled her and her colleagues. She posed different research questions and described a unique database assembled by her project. She pointed out that not one scholar had come to use it or to offer help. "You," she told the committee, "are our only hope." The committee did not formally respond to her request. It did, however, continue with its efforts to organize a conference on policy to include representatives of community action and related projects. A dry run of the conference took place in June 1993, and the conference itself in November.

Only a little more than a month before the committee's research conference, the civil disorders in Los Angeles had erupted following the acquittal of the policemen who beat motorist Rodney King. These events were very much on the minds of conference participants, who alluded to them often. Events in Los Angeles, many felt, had given the committee's subject new urgency. They might bring heightened prominence to its work and attention by policy makers. What the committee would say about the events, however, was less clear. For all the sophistication and technical excellence of its work, it spoke with no unified voice. Even more, with only some notable exceptions, it had avoided direct confrontations with politics, race, and the institutional collapse of the inner city.

Without doubt, the committee stimulated an enormous amount of work on urban poverty; its training programs reached dozens of young scholars who promise to reinvigorate the field; its publications provide reliable data with which to counter stereotypes and facile generalizations about poverty and welfare—but the committee did not directly address the day-to-day struggles of poor people in inner cities, the collapse of institutions and community, or the needs of activists responding to the effects of public and private disinvestment. Its neglect of these subjects was not unique. It reflected the history of modern social science, which, in the interests of "objectivity" and professionalism, has tried to erect walls between research and advocacy and to assure control of the research agenda by experts usually based within universities.[1] As a consequence, the academic debate on urban poverty and the underclass, sophisticated and useful as are its results, has elided some of the major issues. Here, I want explain how the debate might be reframed in ways that directly address, rather than avoid, the implications of rebellion in Los Angeles and the needs of those who work in the streets of inner cities.

I will try to prod thinking about urban poverty in what seem to me useful directions by asking three questions: How are we to account for the capture of poverty discourse by the concept *underclass*? How new are conditions within inner cities? What happens if we shift the focus of concern from individual behavior and pathology to the way the interaction of politics and economics shapes and reshapes cities, that is, to the political economy of place?

FROM THE "UNDESERVING POOR" TO THE "UNDERCLASS"

In 1977 *Time* magazine announced the emergence of a menacing underclass in America's inner cities. Drugs, crime, teenage pregnancy, and high unemployment, not poverty, defined the underclass, most of whose members were young and minority. "Behind the [ghetto's] crumbling walls," wrote *Time*, "lives a large group of people who are

---

[1] Mary O. Furner, *Advocacy and Objectivity: A Crisis in the Professionalization of American Social Science* (Lexington: University of Kentucky Press, 1975); Robyn Muncy, *Creating a Female Dominion in American Reform, 1860–1935* (New York: Oxford University Press, 1991).

more intractable, more socially alien and more hostile than almost anyone had imagined. They are the unreachables: the American underclass. . . . Their bleak environment nurtures values that are often at odds with those of the majority—even the majority of the poor. Thus the underclass produces a highly disproportionate number of the nation's juvenile delinquents, school dropouts, drug addicts and welfare mothers, and much of the adult crime, family disruption, urban decay and demand for social expenditures."[2]

By the late 1970s, this specter of an emergent underclass permeated discussions of America's inner cities. *Underclass* conjured a mysterious wilderness in the heart of America's cities; a terrain of violence and despair; a collectivity outside politics and social structure, beyond the usual language of class and stratum, unable to protest or revolt.

With the publication of Ken Auletta's *The Underclass* in 1982, the underclass secured its dominance in the vocabulary of inner-city pathology. Auletta reinforced the image emerging in the mass media. His underclass consisted of a relatively permanent minority among the poor who fell into four distinct categories: the passive poor, hostile street criminals, hustlers, and the traumatized.[3] Auletta solidified the definition diffused by the mass media. In this portrait, a new social stratum, identified by a set of interlocking behaviors, not primarily by poverty, dominated the wastelands that were all that remained of America's urban-industrial heartland. In the words of prominent political theorist James Q. Wilson, "Despite the efforts of some to discourage the use of the word 'underclass,' it is nonsense to pretend that such a group does not exist or is not a threat. The reason why it is called an underclass and why we worry about it is that its members have a bad character: They mug, do drugs, desert children, and scorn education."[4]

Many commentators have questioned the adequacy and usefulness of this conception of an underclass, and I count myself among its strong critics. For a historian, however, the first question is not how

[2] "The American Underclass," *Time*, August 29, 1977, pp. 14–17.

[3] Ken Auletta, *The Underclass* (New York: Random House, 1982).

[4] James Q. Wilson, "Redefining Equality: The Liberalism of Mickey Kaus," *Public Interest*, no. 109 (fall 1992): 101–8, quote on p. 103.

well *underclass* captures a segment of inner-city experience but why it has gained such prominence. Why, at this moment in American history, have so many commentators eagerly, often unreflectively, appropriated *underclass* as shorthand for describing the population of inner cities? One reason is that *underclass* is not really a sociological term but a convenient metaphor for use in commentaries on inner-city crises. As a metaphor, *underclass* evokes three widely shared perceptions: novelty, complexity, and danger. Conditions within inner cities are unprecedented; they cannot be reduced to a single factor; and they menace the rest of us.

Underclass is a metaphor for the social transformation embedded in these perceptions. Because so many people share these perceptions, *underclass* has become the idiom for discussions of crises in inner cities. "Why are neighborhoods, schools, and public spaces so difficult to make part of a class-mixing public sphere?" asks Mickey Kaus in his widely discussed book, *The End of Equality*. "There are reasons peculiar to each institution. . . . But there is one factor common to all: fear of the 'ghetto poor' underclass." In discussing the underclass, "the problem we are talking about," Kaus contends, "is the culture of our largely black (and largely urban) ghettos. . . . It is the part [of the problem] that poses the greatest threat to the public sphere and social equality."[5]

One strand of this metaphor—the novelty of the underclass—remains more contentious than the others. Is there, in fact, an unprecedented configuration of poverty and related problems within today's cities? Or, as Nicholas Lemann asserts, do contemporary inner cities embody "really an old problem that has become more isolated and concentrated and, as a result, gotten worse and more obvious"?[6] Some commentators deny that an unprecedented set of conditions afflicts poor people in America's inner cities. They worry that arguments for a new underclass represent a resurgence of old images of the undeserving poor, an attempt to mask the recurrent, grinding poverty generated by the working of the economy and social system with an

[5] Mickey Kaus, *The End of Equality* (New York: Basic Books, 1992), pp. 103, 106.

[6] Nicholas Lemann, *The Promised Land: The Great Black Migration and How It Changed America* (New York: Alfred A. Knopf, 1991), p. 344

65

argument that blames the victim and justifies harsh, punitive responses. How do they reach these conclusions? Their case for continuity rests on a reading of both the history of ideas about poverty and the history of social conditions in America's cities.

Proponents of continuity stress the connection between current descriptions of the underclass and discussions of urban poverty throughout the last two centuries. They point out correctly that evidence of ideological persistence abounds and that the language of the underclass echoes the oldest themes in American discussions of urban poverty. One of these very old themes is the division of poor people into moral categories.

Attempts to divide poor people into categories and to distinguish invidiously among them go back centuries. Before the late-eighteenth and early-nineteenth centuries, poor-law officials tried to distinguish between the "able-bodied" and "impotent" poor. The distinction reflected the need to distribute scarce resources rather than moral judgment. In practice, however, no one could draw the line with precision. Faced with increases in poverty and expenses for poor relief, nineteenth-century writers moralized the old distinction between the impotent and able-bodied poor into the worthy and unworthy or deserving and undeserving.[7]

By the second quarter of the nineteenth century, the moralization of the ancient distinction between the able-bodied and impotent poor had injected the vocabulary of poverty with two of its lasting features: the division of the poor into categories of merit and the assumption that the roots of poverty lay in individual misbehavior. Writing about poverty by the political Left as well as the Right frequently reflected these ideas. Marxists talked about the lumpenproletariat, and even reformers in the Progressive Era who began to criticize individual explanations of poverty in the 1890s used the old distinctions. Insofar as it is described in moral terms, the underclass falls within this tradition.

[7] The discussion here draws on my book *The Undeserving Poor: From the War on Poverty to the War on Welfare* (New York: Pantheon, 1989) and on my introduction and conclusion to my edited volume *The "Underclass" Debate: Views from History* (Princeton: Princeton University Press, 1993). Full citations may be found in those sources.

As in contemporary discussions, nineteenth-century proto–social scientists and reformers complained about incompetent parenting and family pathology among the poor, and they worried that the undeserving poor clustered in inner cities where they formed slums that threatened to infect both the respectable poor and the middle classes. Stripped of its period features, nineteenth-century discussions of inner cities sound remarkably contemporary. Observers worried, as they do today, about the consequences of social isolation and the growing concentration of poverty. In 1854, in his first annual report as head of New York City's Children's Aid Society, Charles Loring Brace argued that the growing density of America's cities had eroded the character of their inhabitants. "The very *condensing* of their number within a small space, seems to stimulate their bad tendencies." He defined the "greatest danger" to America's future as "the existence of an ignorant, debased, and permanently poor class in the great cities. . . . The members of it come at length to form a separate population. They embody the lowest passions and the most thriftless habits of the community. They corrupt the lowest class of working-poor who are around them. The expenses of police, of prisoners, of charities and means of relief, arise mainly from them."[8]

Later in the century, reformers argued that the unsanitary, congested housing of the poor bred immorality, crime, and disease. Slums, they argued, were viruses that infected the moral and physical health of the city districts that surrounded them. "We must deal with [pauperism]," claimed New York City's Charity Organization Society in 1886, "as we would with a malarial swamp, draining and purifying it instead of walling it about, or its miasma will spread and taint neighborhoods like a plague."[9] In the writing of nineteenth-century urban reformers, urban poverty acquired its lasting association with disease, embodied most recently in the melding of drugs, AIDS, social isolation, and concentrated poverty into metaphors of an epidemic threatening to leap the boundaries of the inner city.[10]

[8] *Second Annual Report of the Children's Aid Society of New York* (New York, 1855), p. 3.

[9] *Fourth Annual Report of the Central Council of the Charity Organization Society of the City of New York, January 1st, 1886* (New York Central Office, 1886), p. 14.

[10] Charles Rosenberg, "What is an Epidemic? AIDS in Historical Perspective," *Daedalus* 118, no. 2 (1989): 1–17.

By the latter-nineteenth century poverty, crime, and disease blended to form a powerful, frightening, and enduring image. As is the case today, its dimensions were novelty, complexity, and danger. Among the urban poor, an undeserving subset, dependent on account of their own shiftless, irresponsible, immoral behavior, burdened honest taxpayers with the cost of their support, threatened their safety, and corrupted the working poor. Increasingly concentrated within slum districts, they lived in growing social isolation, cut off from the role models and oversight once provided by the more well-to-do, reproducing their own degradation.

Social policy had failed to prevent the emergence of the late-nineteenth century's version of the underclass. Poorhouses, for instance, the core policy innovation of the early-nineteenth century, as I observed in chapter 1, had met none of their sponsors' goals. Despised, neglected, they moved to the backwaters of social policy, increasingly transformed by the removal of special classes of inmates (children, the mentally ill, and the sick) into public old-age homes. Public school systems, once the hope of urban reformers, had developed into huge, unresponsive bureaucracies (see chapter 3) that, critics argued, delivered education less effectively than the smaller schools of the past. Riddled with graft, outdoor relief (public welfare) demoralized the poor and fueled a meteoric rise in taxes. For more than a century, Americans, with good reason, have wondered why social policies and institutions so often have seemed to fail and whether they did more harm than good.

As reformers and legislators cast about for new policies, they did not abandon the distinction between the deserving and the undeserving poor. Nor did they redefine its dimensions. The deserving poor fell into two classes: first, clearly helpless and pathetic people who on account of age or infirmity could neither care for nor support themselves. The other class met dual criteria: circumstances beyond their own responsibility (the death of a husband or a seasonal layoff, for instance) rendered them dependent *and* they proved themselves willing to work for whatever small support public and private charity might offer. Most deserving were widows who kept their children clean, taught them manners, sent them to school, managed their meager incomes effectively, and spent hours every day sewing or scrubbing for tiny wages. The other able-bodied poor were family men out of work, sober and responsible, willing to chop wood or break stone. However, they remained, always, slightly suspect because they had failed to save for the episodes of dependence that predictably punctuated life among the working class.[11]

In their emphasis on race, gender, and culture, the great themes in late-nineteenth-century discussions of urban poverty also resemble those in contemporary writing about the underclass. In popular impressions (although not in fact), the color of the underclass is black. Despite the continuing racism that has scarred American history, this association of urban poverty with race is relatively new, a product of the massive migration of African Americans into northern and midwestern cities after World War II. Before then, of course, most African Americans lived in rural areas, and racial ghettos within northern cities remained relatively small. At the time, the most visible extreme poverty occurred within the vast tenement-house districts inhabited by second-generation whites and new European immigrants. Nonetheless, observers very often framed discussions of poverty in racial terms, which they applied to nationality groups. This "scientific racism" culminated in the eugenics movements and, in the 1920s, immigration restriction.

In the 1960s, writers who tried to interpret the growth and persistence of poverty formalized long-standing arguments about behavioral pathology into a theory of culture, which, despite shifts in its political connotation, has proved remarkably tenacious. Anthropologist Oscar Lewis injected the "culture of poverty" into academic social science and popular commentary. The culture of poverty both echoed old ideas and prefigured future debates. It also meshed with developments in social psychology and reflected the assumption, widespread among liberal intellectuals, of the helplessness and passivity of dependent peoples, who needed the assistance of outsiders to break the cycles of deprivation and degradation that reproduced it from generation to generation. The culture of poverty also offered a

[11] My conclusions here rest on my reading of case records of nineteenth-century philanthropic agencies.

more palatable explanation than false consciousness of why very poor
people failed to revolt, or even protest, and why so many remained
unmoved by the rising tide of postwar affluence.[12]

Lewis and others who adapted the culture of poverty to particular
issues, such as education, where "cultural deprivation" enjoyed a
short vogue as an explanation for learning problems, hoped to put
the idea to liberal political purposes as a force energizing activist, in-
terventionist public policy.[13] They did not intend to reproduce the old
distinction between the worthy and unworthy poor. Nonetheless, others with more conservative agendas turned the concept's original politics on its head. The culture of poverty became a euphemism for the
pathology of the undeserving poor, an explanation for their condition,
an excuse, as in the writing of Edward Banfield, for both inaction and
harsh, punitive public policy.[14]

The culture of poverty fused with racial politics in 1965 with the leak
of a confidential report to President Lyndon Johnson by a young assistant secretary of labor. Daniel Patrick Moynihan's *Negro Family: The
Case for National Action* did not use the phrase "culture of poverty,"
but its language, especially its metaphor "tangle of pathology,"
seemed to reflect the same ideas. Moynihan actually grounded his
analysis of the development of single-parent black families in the unemployment of black men, a fact most of his critics overlooked. Nonetheless, he identified the fundamental problem within black communities as "family structure" (meaning out-of-wedlock births, female
headship, and welfare dependence) and warned of the grave consequences of the dominance of a black "matriarchy." [15]

[12] Lee Rainwater, "The Problem of Lower Class Culture," *Journal of Social Issues* 26
(1970): 133–37; Oscar Handlin, *Boston's Immigrants, 1790–1865: A Study in Acculturation*,
rev. and enl. ed. (Cambridge: Harvard University Press, 1959), pp. 51, 120–21, 125;
Stanley M. Elkins, *Slavery: A Problem in American Institutional Life*, 3d ed. (Chicago: University of Chicago Press, 1976); David C. McClelland, *The Achieving Society* (New York:
Free Press, 1961), pp. 36, 43, 205.

[13] Frank Riessman, *The Culturally Deprived Child* (New York: Harper and Row,
1962).

[14] Edward Banfield, *The Unheavenly City* (Boston: Little, Brown, 1970).

[15] For the text of the Moynihan report and an excellent selection of responses, see Lee
Rainwater and William L. Yancey, *The Moynihan Report and the Politics of Controversy*
(Cambridge: MIT Press, 1967).

Moynihan's report coincided with the crest of the Civil Rights Movement, and civil rights leaders and others found Moynihan's analysis, as reported in the press, offensive, empirically flawed, denigrating, deflecting blame from the sources of poverty to its victims. The furor over Moynihan's report, in fact, drove black families off the agenda of mainstream social science for nearly two decades. Similar attacks discredited the culture of poverty.

By and large, intellectuals did not provide a fresh or useful foundation for alternative policies or research that asked new questions. In fact, a long intellectual tradition views the poor (except for clever paupers who play the system) as demoralized and denuded of the will and capacity for constructive self-help. This one major theme runs from the early-nineteenth-century commentary on the inner-city poor to the contemporary view of the underclass. It is one reason why poverty research has focused more on pathology than on politics, more on improving poor people and their behavior than on places and the reclamation of urban space.

For the most part, the assumptions of the War on Poverty during the same years fit within the prevailing framework. Only community action—the emphasis on the participation of the poor in the design and implementation of programs to serve them—rejected conventional approaches. The most controversial portion of the poverty war, community action challenged the power of state and local politicians, who quickly goaded Congress and the president into blunting its impact and denaturing its meaning. For the most part, the War on Poverty rested firmly on supply-side views of poverty. It emphasized opportunity, not through focusing on the labor market, as the Department of Labor at first advocated, but through improving individual skills with education and job training.[16] The lack of coordination between welfare and labor-market policy has continued to undermine federal anti-

[16] Margaret Weir, "The Federal Government and Unemployment: The Frustration of Policy Innovation from the New Deal to the Great Society," in Margaret Weir et al., eds., *The Politics of Social Policy in the United States* (Princeton: Princeton University Press, 1988); "Poverty and Urban Policy: Transcript of 1973 Group Discussion of the Kennedy Administration Urban Poverty Programs and Policies," John Fitzgerald Kennedy Archives, Boston; Katz, *Undeserving Poor*, pp. 79–123.

poverty efforts. For reasons that are difficult to understand, the two policy streams usually have operated independently of one another. Some exceptions at the state level do exist, but as a general rule this lack of coordination has severely hindered programs that sought to move people from welfare to self-sufficiency.[17]

Nonetheless, in the 1960s and early 1970s, the War on Poverty, the Great Society, and expansion of social welfare assisted poor people by increasing the availability of services and raising benefits. Operation Headstart, the Legal Services Program, food stamps, Medicare, Medicaid, the Jobs Corps, higher Social Security benefits, and Supplemental Social Security improved the lives of a great many of the urban poor. In the same years, civil rights legislation facilitated the entrance of African Americans into middle-class employment, especially in the public sector, and poverty among African Americans dropped sharply. For instance, between 1959 and 1979, poverty among fully employed blacks declined from 43 percent to 16 percent.[18] President Ronald Reagan once said that America fought a war on poverty and that poverty won. His statement misrepresented history. For one thing, it ignored the very real achievements of the federal government, such as cutting poverty among the elderly by two-thirds, expanding the supply of public housing, improving nutrition, and increasing medical assistance to poor people. For another, it implied the impotence of the federal government and cast doubts on its competence. Not only has the federal government proven its ability to mount effective programs (although, of course, it is better at some sorts of programs than at others), in truth, for good or ill, the federal government always impacts the lives of the poor, either directly or through setting limits and possibilities. The federal government remains potentially the most powerful weapon in the anti-poverty arsenal.

[17] On the failure of labor-market policy, see the important study by Margaret Weir, *Politics and Jobs: The Boundaries of Employment Policy in the United States* (Princeton: Princeton University Press, 1992); the welfare reform program in Massachusetts, known as E.T., successfully coordinated welfare and labor policy; at present, the Commonwealth of Pennsylvania's New Directions program is an example of a current effort to coordinate them.

[18] Mark J. Stern, "Poverty and Family Composition since 1940," in Katz, "*Underclass*" *Debate*, p. 223.

By and large, academic economists of the 1970s did not consider the implications of their research for assessing the distinction between the deserving and undeserving poor and its relation to the existence of a culture of poverty. By the early 1980s, however, conservative writers drew the connection. The question, asked in the conservative political climate of the era, was this: Why, despite all the new social programs of the War on Poverty and the Great Society, had poverty worsened? What explained the explosive growth of female-headed African American families, the unemployment of African American men, and the crime, violence, and social disorganization within inner cities? Spending on social welfare had risen dramatically; segregation and other barriers to African American economic and political advancement had lowered; the country had enjoyed unusual prosperity and economic growth. Given this context, what could account for the rise in social pathology, especially among inner-city African Americans?[19]

Conservatives placed the blame on welfare and government social programs, which, they argued, had demoralized the poor by eroding incentives to work, undermining family stability, and nurturing a self-perpetuating culture of dependence. Although social scientists subjected conservative writing to withering attacks, the conservatives had tapped the issues that troubled many Americans and had offered clear answers. Many remained predisposed to believe them, despite evidence to the contrary. Indeed, for the most part, liberal social scientists failed to move beyond criticism of data and methods. They addressed themselves to the same questions about the results of welfare and offered different answers. But they could say little in answer to the basic questions posed by conservatives.[20]

Conservatives supplied the intellectual mortar for a war on welfare at each level of government—local, state, and federal. In retrospect, the response to New York City's fiscal crisis in the mid-1970s represented the first assault. There, government pioneered in the applica-

[19] Charles Murray, *Losing Ground: American Social Policy, 1950–1980* (New York: Basic Books, 1984); George Gilder, *Wealth and Poverty* (New York: Basic Books, 1981).

[20] Robert Greenstein, "Losing Faith in *Losing Ground*," *New Republic*, March 25, 1985, p. 14; Christopher Jencks, "How Poor Are the Poor?" *New York Review* 32 (May 5, 1985): 41.

tion of austerity measures to reduce a massive deficit. With public officials and private commentators heaping responsibility for the deficit on allegedly extravagant public salaries and benefits, selfish unions, and municipal inefficiency, the responsibility of banks that had encouraged the city to pile up debts and then refused to roll over bonds faded from view, except among writers on the political Left. As the state-appointed fiscal oversight boards, which removed effective financial authority from the voters to representatives of business and the state, encouraged the city government to slash institutions that served poor people, such as health clinics and day-care centers, and fire thousands of modestly paid municipal workers, it underwrote new bonds for which existing city bondholders could exchange their notes and earn higher interest rates.[21]

The second assault on welfare occurred in state governments in the form of campaigns against General Assistance. A modest program offering minimal benefits to individuals eligible for no other public help, General Assistance inherited the historic opprobrium attached to outdoor relief. To its critics, its recipients were the undeserving poor. The campaign against General Assistance, launched in Massachusetts in 1975, spread throughout the country, gathering strength during the 1980s and into the 1990s. Where, as in Pennsylvania, legislative action successfully reduced General Assistance, destitution and suffering increased with no reduction in the public expense, individual dependence, or unemployment that the measure's sponsors had predicted.

With the election of Ronald Reagan in 1980, the federal government's war on welfare, like New York City's an exercise in regressive austerity, gathered both ideological momentum and practical force. Trotting out the oldest, most discredited stereotypes of welfare and its clients, polishing romantic myths about the role of voluntarism in

[21] Roger E. Alcaly and David Mermelstein, *The Fiscal Crisis of American Cities: Essays on the Political Economy of Urban American with Special Reference to New York* (New York: Random House, 1977); William K. Tabb, *The Long Default: New York City and the Urban Fiscal Crisis* (New York: Monthly Review Press, 1982); Martin Shefter, *Political Crisis/Fiscal Crisis: The Collapse and Revival of New York City* (New York: Basic Books, 1985).

meeting social needs, Reagan's government attacked social spending. Although it failed to gut programs to the extent it wanted, it did rip massive holes in the social safety net, virtually terminating the construction of public housing, starving cities for funds, eliminating a number of programs, and excluding people from benefits by tightening administrative regulations. (Federal funds to cities, for instance, were slashed nearly in half.)[22] Some of the results may be seen in the crumbling infrastructure and on the streets of every major American city. At the same time, of course, the administration's tax policies gave the rich an enormous windfall, some of whose results also are visible on city streets, wafting upward into luxury office buildings and condominiums rather than, as promised, trickling downward to those in need.

In the 1980s, the conservative theories underlying the war on welfare encountered little serious or powerful opposition. When the underclass surfaced in *Time*, other magazines, and Auletta's book, few liberal social scientists objected. They had no alternative framework. With no other language in which to describe or comprehend what had happened within inner cities, the underclass became a new neutral ground on which to debate. What were its characteristics? Its sources? Its prognosis? As leading liberal social scientists tried to appropriate the concept from both the media and conservative commentary, they faced one especially delicate obstacle. How could they reinsert culture and the African American family onto the agenda of social science without conceding the argument to the conservatives? No realistic analysis of inner-city poverty could ignore family, which, in fact, had emerged as a key concern within African American communities. But in politics and social science, conservatives had appropriated family and culture in the 1960s.

The major liberal response came in 1987 with William Julius Wilson's *Truly Disadvantaged*, which tried to incorporate family and culture into a social-democratic analysis of inner-city poverty and the underclass. Wilson worried about the growth of single-parent fami-

[22] Demetrios Caraley, "Washington Abandons the Cities," *Political Science Quarterly* 107 (spring 1992): 1–30.

lies, whose consequences he described in terms not unlike those used by conservatives, except he attributed declining marriage rates and out-of-wedlock births among African Americans to the massive and growing labor-force detachment of young men, which he explained by the transformation of the economic base, social structure, and spatial organization of cities. *The Truly Disadvantaged* quickly became the most influential scholarly book on contemporary American poverty.[23] Wilson presented *The Truly Disadvantaged* as a series of hypotheses based on the best evidence available at the time, and he mounted a large research project to test his ideas. As other social scientists followed his lead, *The Truly Disadvantaged* also set the agenda for the first round of research on the urban underclass.

Wilson and others influenced by him assumed that the underclass resulted from patterns of poverty unique in the history of American cities. However, poverty has pervaded American cities throughout their history, including in periods commonly remembered as prosperous. Throughout modern American history poor people have clustered together in the neighborhoods of American cities. By any reasonable standards, around half of New York City's population was poor in 1900. The same, undoubtedly, was the case in other large cities. With work unsteady and wages low, many city people never escaped poverty even though they managed to sustain themselves and their families most of the time without charity or public assistance. The main dividing line separated the poor from the dependent, those managing by themselves from those in need of help. In practice, many crossed back and forth between self-sufficiency and dependence during the periods of predictable crises and emergencies that punctuated working-class lives.[24]

As for African Americans, scholars from W. E. B. Dubois in the late-nineteenth century to Roger Lane today have written about crime, violence, and large numbers of female-headed families within America's

---

[23] William J. Wilson, *The Truly Disadvantaged: The Inner City, the Underclass, and Public Policy* (Chicago: University of Chicago Press, 1987).

[24] See chapt. 4; also Alexander Keyssar, *Out of Work: The First Century of Unemployment in Massachusetts* (New York: Cambridge University Press, 1986).

early urban ghettos, although the numbers did not reach anything like their current heights.[25] What, then, is new? Although problems may have worsened in recent years, have their contours remained essentially the same? The answer is no. The situation within today's inner cities is unprecedented. Nonetheless, we confront this new situation with an old vocabulary and shopworn ideas—one reason why discussions of poverty often sound so stale, repetitive, and unhelpful.

POVERTY AND THE POSTINDUSTRIAL CITY

Understanding why the situation in today's inner cities is novel starts with the observation that poverty, racism, and social disorganization are in part social constructions, not fixed, objective categories. They are ways of representing relations among individuals, groups, institutions, and their settings. Their shifting contours and meanings have reflected changing social, economic, political, and intellectual contexts. In recent decades the emergence of the postindustrial city dramatically and irrevocably has transformed these contexts and with them the meaning of poverty, race, and social disorganization.

Three transformations have shaped postindustrial cities: the transformation of their economy, demography, and space. The economic transformation consists of the replacement of manufacturing with services, especially in formerly industrial cities now characterized more by the production of information than goods, and to the new, increasingly bifurcated occupational structure that supports this emergent urban role. Demographic transformation refers to various processes: depopulation, the replacement of whites primarily of European ancestry with African Americans, Latinos, and new immigrants, the increased proportion of residents who are poor, and the much larger numbers of both young adults living apart from their families and female-headed families. Spatial transformation includes suburbanization, heightened segregation, increased concentrations of poverty, the

[25] W. E. B. Du Bois, *The Philadelphia Negro: A Social History* (1899; reprint, New York: Shocken Books, 1967); Roger Lane, *The Roots of Violence in Black Philadelphia, 1860–1900* (Cambridge: Harvard University Press, 1986).

revitalization of downtowns and the decay of neighborhoods, the balkanization of districts through the location of freeways and public housing, and gentrification. All these changes, which are intricately connected, have combined to create an urban form unlike any other in history.

Because of these transformations, the experience, meaning, and implications of poverty in today's cities differ from the poverty of the past on three dimensions: the opportunity context for the poor, their relation to the labor market, and the spatial distribution of poverty. The poverty of earlier periods coexisted with expanding opportunity and urban growth as unskilled and semiskilled work in cities increased throughout America's industrialization. Large industries, in fact, provided steadier work, better wages, and limited hierarchies that working people could climb. As a result, expanding opportunities opened modest avenues for social mobility. The wages of employed family members might be combined to buy property; steady employment might lead to higher pay within a factory; with the help of schooling, children could improve on the status of their parents. These processes worked imperfectly; dramatic mobility remained rare; simply getting by continued to be difficult for most working people. Still, over time real wages rose, most ethnic groups improved their living conditions, and their rate of poverty decreased. Poverty existed within a context of hope.

All this has changed for the mostly minority populations who remain in inner cities. Deindustrialization and depopulation, not growth, shape the new context. Very few opportunities exist for industrial work. Government jobs, one avenue toward economic security and mobility for African Americans, have shrunk. For the most part, new jobs in the service sector divide into those which pay well but demand more education than most minorities acquire and those which offer part-time, nonunion work that pays badly. The value of public benefits directed exclusively to poor people has eroded, many programs have been scaled back or cut, and the construction of public housing almost ceased during the 1980s. Although more muted, racism continues as well to limit the opportunities of African Americans, especially men who confront employers unwilling to hire them.

"America's version of *apartheid*," observes political scientist Andrew Hacker, "while lacking overt legal sanction, comes closest to the system even now being reformed in the land of its invention."[26] Poverty now increasingly exists within a context of hopelessness.

Excluding those who could not work on account of infirmity or age, in earlier periods dependence (which I use in contrast to poverty, because low wages kept so many workers poor) resulted when people lost work, usually temporarily, often in slack seasons or economic downturns. Now, especially among minorities in inner cities (and despite the growing number of working poor), poverty and dependence denote detachment from the labor force. They are the statuses associated with a very large number of people who do not work (at least in the regular economy), who have not worked for a long time, who may, in fact, never have worked, and whose prospects for employment grow increasingly dim. Although the proportion of African Americans who are poor has declined steeply since the 1960s, the number who are chronically without jobs has risen sharply. As a result, the chronically jobless compose an ever larger share of the poor, and African Americans constitute a greater share of those chronically without jobs now than in earlier periods. This connection between race, urban poverty, and dissociation from the labor market is new in American history.

The problem extends beyond joblessness. Between 1940 and 1980, the gap in wages between black and white males decreased, largely as a result of increased schooling among blacks. Remaining differences in wages, observers predicted, ultimately would disappear along with disparities in educational attainment. In the 1980s, however, wage inequality between black and white men increased at all educational levels. The reason, according to one recent study, is the price of "skill," especially basic math and reading ability, which rose during the 1980s. When controlled for measured skill, the value of a high school degree became insignificant. Among men with more than a high school education, growing wage inequality between blacks and whites also reflected differences in measured skill, or, looked at another way, in the

---

[26] Andrew Hacker, *Two Nations: Black and White, Separate, Hostile, Unequal*, (New York: Charles Scribner's Sons, 1992), p. 4.

effectiveness of their educations. As educational credentials by themselves lost credibility as certificates of competence, the differences in the quality of education received by blacks and whites reinforced patterns of racial inequality. This is another way in which new labor-market contexts have eroded opportunity structures for African Americans.[27]

The spatial distribution of poverty in postindustrial American cities also is new. Nineteenth-century commentators who reported growing concentrations of poverty in American cities worried about an increasing lack of contact between rich and poor, and their images prefigured the rhetoric of the underclass literature today. In fact, spatial differentiation remained far muddier than it is in contemporary cities. In the era before inexpensive and convenient mass transportation, rich and poor lived for the most part in close proximity as poor people clustered into pockets and alleyways near the homes of the affluent. This is the clear conclusion of social historians who have reconstructed urban neighborhoods.

Racial ghettos began to develop even before the Great Migration of the post–World War I era. They were the seeds from which contemporary patterns of racial isolation grew. With African Americans comprising a relatively low proportion of urban populations until the decades following World War II, they nonetheless remained in generally small pockets within diverse cities, and indexes of segregation stood far lower than they are now. Early in the twentieth century, European immigrants lived in more segregated neighborhoods than did African Americans. Indeed, the spreading concentration of districts both poor and black within today's cities, the ecological foundation of the underclass, stands without precedent in America's history.

In a book of extraordinary importance, *American Apartheid*, Douglas S. Massey and Nancy A. Denton demonstrate the persistence of segregation and show how segregation perpetuates poverty. Both "unprecedented and utterly unique," black segregation, they point out,

---

[27] Ronald F. Ferguson, "New Evidence on the Growing Value of Skill and Consequences for Racial Disparity and Returns to Schooling" (unpublished paper #H-93-10, Malcolm Wiener Center for Social Policy, John F. Kennedy School of Government, Harvard University, September 1993).

"shows little sign of change with the passage of time or improvements in socioeconomic status." Segregation matters because it "is not a neutral fact; it systematically undermines the social and economic well-being of blacks in the United States." The "deleterious" conditions in black neighborhoods "occur because segregation concentrates poverty to build a set of mutually reinforcing and self-feeding spirals of decline." As jobs disappear in segregated neighborhoods, poverty becomes more concentrated, "creating uniquely disadvantaged environments that become progressively isolated—geographically, socially, and economically—from the rest of society."[28] Nothing comparable has happened before in American history.

Using measures of segregation, an observer could conclude that the situation of blacks in American cities has worsened. By focusing on trends in poverty or educational attainment, another observer could conclude that their circumstances have improved. Neither would be incorrect, but both would be asking the wrong question. In fact, too many writers cast their stories about race, poverty, and welfare in terms of progress or decline. For Mickey Kaus, the important story is how welfare produced an underclass by undermining work and family. For Lawrence Mead, it is a paradox: improving economic and social conditions accompanied by deteriorating behavior, most notably willful joblessness. For Andrew Hacker, it is the social consequences of worsening race relations. Even for William Julius Wilson, a sophisticated analyst, declension from a golden age of interclass relations within ghettos remains central to his interpretation of current inner-city problems. Among current writers, Christopher Jencks partially escapes the conventional frame by showing how various measures improved or worsened in recent decades. Nonetheless, this question—Are things getting better or worse?—also drove his analysis, even though his answer is complex. As in old-fashioned Whig history, a preoccupation with progress or its opposite abstracts the story of race, poverty, or welfare from its context. It measures by standards of the present, misses the conditioning of ideas and policies by their setting, misreads surface similarities as fundamental identities, and trans-

---

[28] Douglas A. Massey and Nancy A. Denton, *American Apartheid: Segregation and the Making of the Underclass* (Cambridge: Harvard University Press, 1993), p. 2.

forms a complicated story into a straight line that misrepresents historical process. It also deflects attention from the task of sorting out the continuities and discontinuities in the history of events, institutions, ideas, and policies. With urban poverty, which I have considered in this chapter, it elides the most important observation: the new experience of poverty occasioned by the transformation of America's inner cities.

POVERTY, POLITICS, AND RESEARCH

Throughout modern American history, great social and economic processes shaped the experience of poverty. With the urban transformations that gave rise to the postindustrial city, each of them intensified. One result was the configuration some observers have labeled the underclass. At the same time, the situation of contemporary inner cities and the people who live in them cannot be understood without reference to politics and the actions of government. The situation signified by "underclass" did not just happen; its emergence was not inevitable. Like the postindustrial city of which it is a part, it is the product of actions and decisions over a very long span of time.

Until the mid-1960s, city, state, and federal governments did little to slow or reverse the processes that resulted in the emergence of concentrated and persistent poverty, especially among African Americans in America's inner cities. To the contrary, from the Constitution's acceptance of slavery through the neighborhood devastation wrought by urban renewal, local, state, and federal governments often contributed to processes of marginalization, exclusion, and isolation. This is not to say that government policies always worked against the interests of the disadvantaged or that government lacks the capacity to reduce poverty, improve housing, lessen hunger, and extend medical care. Beginning with the accomplishments of the New Deal in the 1930s, social programs often succeeded, and many researchers have documented the major gains of the period from the early 1960s to, roughly, 1973.

Nonetheless, government actions have intensified both the spread of poverty and the decline of formerly great cities. Consider the following as brief examples: in the 1930s, federal agricultural policy, embodied in the Agricultural Adjustment Act, hurt small and often black farmers by allowing large planters to displace them with government subsidies for uncultivated land. In the same years, by introducing "redlining" into mortgage appraisal practices, the Federal Housing Authority hastened the deterioration of city neighborhoods by starving them of capital for home ownership. Federal highway policy built expressways that destroyed housing, helped empty cities of their middle classes, and sealed off minority areas. Federal urban renewal programs did not rehouse the great majority of the residents whose homes they tore down in order to revive downtowns with new office towers and commercial space. Governments at all levels colluded to transform much public housing into stigmatized, segregated, underfunded ghettos.

In the 1960s, the War on Poverty and the expansion of related government programs created poverty research as a field in social science because legislation mandated evaluation. Leadership fell to economics, which alone among the social sciences seemed to offer the necessary tools, theories, and prestige. Criticisms of the "culture of poverty," which culminated in attacks on the Moynihan report, tarnished sociology and anthropology, which had failed to develop compelling alternative perspectives on poverty or ways of answering legislators' and administrators' questions about the results of programs. Policy research itself became a new field, grounded in economics, located within new schools in universities and in the new world of independent centers and institutes. Poverty researchers developed sophisticated new methods, especially large-scale social experiments, applied most notably to tests of income maintenance programs, but they contributed few new ideas and little in the way of theory. Poverty research revolved, in fact, around one of the oldest preoccupations in the history of poverty and welfare: the results of relief. Did welfare hurt the labor market by weakening the willingness to work? Did it erode family life? Did it demoralize the poor? These questions, as chapter 1 observed, drove the poor-law debates of the late-eighteenth and early-nineteenth centuries; they energized the expensive and inconclusive research into income maintenance and other ex-

CHAPTER TWO

perimental programs in the late 1960s and early 1970s; and they
fueled the evaluations of "workfare" in the 1980s. Both the political
Left and Right accepted them as the key questions; only their answers
differed.

The questions driving the round of research on the underclass that
started in the late 1980s differed in some ways, but they still focused
primarily on behavior. The main issues have been these: the extent to
which individuals are responsible for their own poverty, or the balance between individual agency and structural forces; the role of culture (defined as the influence of sets of attitudes, values, and group
behaviors) on perpetuating poverty and dependence; the contribution
of family structure, organization, and modes of child rearing to developing and reproducing social pathologies; the influence of ecology, or
environment, on behavior (put another way, how neighborhood characteristics contribute to crime, welfare dependence, low school attendance, and premarital pregnancy); and the conundrum of why poverty persists despite public policy and whether policy has, in fact,
made matters worse. More recently, attention has begun to focus on
why black men do so badly in the labor market.[29]

By contrast, ethnographers and social historians have tried to
change the questions underlying poverty research. One of their great
recent services has been redrawing the portrait of ordinary city people. In place of demoralization and passivity, they have described
their survival strategies, the resilience of their families, and their distinctive politics. (I return to this topic in chapter 4.) Although disparities in power and resources have limited the achievements of poor
people, despite those constraints a history of action on their own be-
half stretches from enslaved people's acts of resistance on plantations
to protests in welfare offices in the 1960s and to the creation of institutions, especially the black church, which, starting in the nineteenth
century, played a prominent role in the struggles against slavery and
for civil rights.[30]

[29] Philip Moss and Chris Tilly, *Why Black Men Are Doing Worse in the Labor Market: A
Review of Supply-Side and Demand-Side Explanations* (New York: Social Science Research
Council, 1991).

[30] Robin D. G. Kelley, "The Black Poor and the Politics of Opposition in a New South
City, 1929–1970," in Katz, *"Underclass" Debate*, pp. 293–333.

As for family, although very large differences still separate whites from blacks on all measures of family structure, trends within African American and white families, such as the increase in female-headed families, run in the same directions. (From 1960 to 1990, households headed by women increased from 24.4 to 56.2 percent among blacks and from 7.3 to 17.3 percent among whites.) Because the same pressures have reshaped all families, black, Latino, and white, the story of underclass families is not unique; it cannot be told without reference to the rest of America. The issue is not what has happened to the black, Latino, or underclass family. Rather, the questions are: What are the forces that underlie massive family change in late-twentieth-century America? Why do they buffet some groups more strongly than others? How do the same pressures translate into rates of family change that vary in different settings? The evidence points in another direction as well. African American families, sustained in part by African cultural traditions, have remained amazingly adaptive and resilient. From forced separation in slavery through the cumulative impact of inner city deterioration and economic restructuring, the often awesome problems confronted by African American families result from the same forces that have eroded inner cities. To hold families responsible for their cause and solution is, in the worst of ways, to blame the victim. Yet this is precisely the direction taken by most recent discussions of welfare reform, which, with near hysterical panic, focus on "illegitimacy" as the source of dependence and other social pathologies. As the rhetoric of Bill Clinton's administration has shown, the transmutation of out-of-wedlock births to poor young women into the root of America's moral rot crosses the lines that otherwise divide political parties. (Nothing more clearly reveals the debased level of public discourse than the readiness of all parties to the welfare debate to label children, indeed, any human beings, as "illegitimate." When most of those dehumanized as "illegitimate" are African Americans, a group formerly denied full humanity by law, the racism underlying the rhetoric of welfare reform loses its technocratic and bureacratic facade.)

I do not propose avoiding the rise in out-of-wedlock births among black women (63.7 percent in 1988, compared to 14.9 percent among whites) or diminishing the poverty and other problems confronting women family heads. Rather, my purpose is to reframe the question, to search for the sources of trends in factors that impinge on all families as well as on the distinctive experience of blacks, to avoid demonizing young black women as the fount of social pathology, the new undeserving poor. Legal theorist Patricia Williams has argued the point with force and clarity:

> The figures indicating an increase in the number of Black single mothers, for example, are too often used by the media to demonize the entire project of Black childbearing and by conservatives to blame some single factor like "welfare dependence." A great deal more might be learned by looking to a range of other conditions affecting the lives of Black women—high infant mortality rates, rape and incest statistics, chronic depression, lack of health care, death by preventable disease, and suicide. And the status of Black single mothers certainly cannot be understood outside of the broader context of data about the lives of Black single men: their mortality rate, their homelessness, rates of arrest, police attacks, incarceration, general unemployment, self-hatred, and homicide. Add into this the greater historic independence of Black women, the general world-wide increase in single motherhood, and one can begin to reconfigure images of shameless promiscuity of wildly proliferating Black women.[31]

Certainly, one question for policy is what can be done to assure women and men who wish to live together and marry the supports they need to maintain a family, or, put negatively and minimally, what can be done to remove the barriers and disincentives that discourage the creation of families. At the same time, given the trends among all women, black and white, working class and professional, policy should also try to break the links between single motherhood and poverty. There is, after all, no inherent reason why single mothers should be poor. Job opportunities, training, day care, health insurance, child support, and, where necessary, wage supplements, I suspect, would erode the alleged culture of dependence more effectively than

[31] Patricia Williams, "The Great Divide," *Tikkun* 7:5 (September/October 1992): 65–68, quote on pp. 67–68.

the coercive mechanisms embedded in the punitive welfare policies that form the leading current strategy for "improving" women in poverty.

Concentration on the family life of the poor obscures another link between them and the rest of America. Poverty signifies a position at the far end of a spectrum of inequality. It is defined in part by its relation to other positions, and its increase indicates a widening of economic distances. The rise in ghetto poverty, therefore, is not an isolated event. Rather, it is the most visible instance of growing income inequality in America, a trend that many researchers have documented for the 1980s. The growth of the working poor is another, less outwardly noticeable example. For this reason, a focus that lingers solely on ghetto poverty distracts attention from its sources in transformations of social structure that threaten the well-being of a very large share of Americans.

The direction of poverty research followed by mainstream American social science did not represent the only available intellectual alternative. In the 1960s, mainly African American intellectuals began to fashion their own explanations for poverty, which could have generated a different and productive research agenda. Black scholars drew from a different intellectual stream to explain the persistence of poverty. Around the globe, previously dependent people were asserting their right to liberation. As they fought guerrilla wars, organized against dictatorships, or, in the United States, struggled against racism and segregation, they revealed the bankruptcy of ideas that portrayed them as passive, incapable of self-assertion, unable to generate indigenous leadership. Their leaders developed theories of dependence and internal colonialism to explain poverty and underdevelopment in the Third World. In radical American writing, the ghetto became a colony and exploitation and racism the explanations for persistent black poverty. Neither the culture of poverty nor the undeserving poor made sense, other than as mystifications that hid the dynamics of power and subordination. This alternative to long-standing themes in American writing about poverty flourished only briefly. Its association with Black Power, location outside the academic mainstream, lack of intel-

87

lectual polish, and the diminishing energy of the Civil Rights Movement all contributed to its failure to alter the framework that constrained discussions of poverty.

POVERTY AND THE POLITICAL ECONOMY OF PLACE

Before its disappearance, the literature of internal colonialism was leading poverty research toward an understanding of how political and economic policies fostered the intensification of urban poverty, that is, toward a political economy of place. Along with historians, scholars who stressed the role of internal colonialism emphasized that African American families always have lived within settings that have impeded the realization of their ideals and goals. More recently, a new urban studies literature has begun to reframe interpretations of poverty and related research agendas by stressing the social construction of space and the political economy of urban decline. Urban decay, it argues, does not reflect the inevitable result of inexorable forces. Rather, it is the legacy of policy and action, of choices and human agency. Urban political history, in fact, tells a story about contests over the definition, ownership, and transformation of space. Urban renewal, highway construction, the underfunding of public transportation, segregation, redlining, disinvestment—all these policies manifest the politics of space that reshaped inner cities.

Signs point to the transmutation of the debate on urban poverty into a broader concern with the regeneration of cities. In its policy conference, the SSRC underclass research committee turned its attention, at last, to the connection between urban revitalization and poverty. Several of the papers it commissioned about policy and programs reported on efforts to revive communities, rebuild institutions, and reclaim urban space. They tapped a vast array of local initiatives throughout the country.[32] Urban questions, conceived more broadly

[32] Good examples are the "program" and "best practices" papers commissioned by the Social Science Research Council's Committee for Research on the Urban Underclass for its policy conference on November 10, 1993. A list of paper titles may be obtained directly from the SSRC, 605 Third Ave., New York, New York 10158.

than as issues of poverty or the underclass, appear to be reemerging as leading concerns of foundations. The federal Department of Housing and Urban Development is searching for strategies that promote urban growth. A nascent academic literature concerns itself with the erosion of the public sphere, the consequences of institutional failure, the importance of civic democracy in social affairs, and the role of "social capital" in the maintenance of viable communities.[33] All these disparate activities assume links among the attenuation of urban social networks, the disappearance or decay of institutions, the disinvestment or flight of capital, and the emergence of new patterns of poverty. The new research cannot always specify those links precisely or identify the most promising strategies for intervention, but, collectively, they furnish the material with which to construct a new, and in important ways more promising, research agenda.

Consider, for example, the work of political scientist Robert D. Putnam on social capital. "Joblessness, inadequate education, and poor health clearly truncate the opportunities of ghetto residents. Yet so do profound deficiencies in social capital," writes Putnam. Drawing on his own research into the conditions of successful civic democracy in Italy as well as on examples from elsewhere in the world, Putnam speculates on the unequal American urban racial and class distribution of the "features of social organization, such as networks, norms, and trust, that facilitate coordination and cooperation for mutual benefit." Measured accurately, these "may be as great as inequalities in financial and human capital, and no less portentous." Putnam's theory implies new directions for urban policy: "investments in physical capital, financial capital, human capital, and social capital are complementary, not competing alternatives. Investments in jobs and education, for example, will be more effective if they are coupled with reinvigoration of community associations."[34]

Along with depleting social capital, the reconstruction of urban space in postindustrial cities has destroyed markets and institutions.

[33] Robert D. Putnam, *Making Democracy Work: Civic Traditions in Modern Italy* (Princeton: Princeton University Press, 1993), pp. 167–71.

[34] Robert D. Putnam, "The Prosperous Community: Social Capital and Public Life," *American Prospect* 13 (spring 1993): 35–42.

In inner cities, neither housing nor jobs function on normal market principles, and market-based policies are unlikely to bring about their transformation. Real-estate developers and landlords cannot earn profits with low-cost housing in areas of concentrated urban poverty; employers find it difficult to recruit a workforce or to offer wages that compete with the illicit economy. At the same time, in areas of concentrated urban poverty the political economy of urban decline has destroyed many institutions, other than those of repression or custody. (The photographer Camilo Jose Vergara has referred to areas of inner cities as the "institutional ghetto.")[35] As forms of "social organization," observes political scientist Gerald Gamm, "neighborhoods at all times require a common network of social interactions. Often that network is crystallized in institutions."[36] Both private and public institutions have abandoned inner cities, destroying the basis of civil society and denuding them of the instruments of collective life. Nonetheless, recent students of inner cities and the underclass by and large have neglected institutions. "Though crucial . . . in any definition of neighborhoods and communities," writes Gamm, "institutions and social networks are virtually absent in studies of neighborhood change," which usually draw on ecological models or "the perverse collective consequences of individual decisions."[37]

Among the obstacles confronting inner-city poor people, the failure of public institutions ranks high because institutions bear directly on every aspect of underclass life. Schools do not educate most of their students; the police have not prevented the escalation of crime, violence, and the use of illegal drugs; the health care system has not reduced the differences in infant mortality between inner cities and suburbs; public welfare rarely helps its clients escape poverty or even survive with minimal comfort and dignity.

This failure of public institutions spreads beyond the underclass or very poor because, as Robert Bellah and his colleagues write, "we live in and through institutions." Americans, they point out, "may experi-

---

[35] Camilo Jose Vergara, "A Guide to the Ghettos," *Nation*, March 15, 1993, pp. 339–42.

[36] Gerald Gamm, "Exodus and Stability: Institutions and Neighborhood Change in Boston, 1948–1993" (paper delivered at annual meeting of American Historical Association, January 1994), p. 14.

[37] Ibid., p. 16.

ence the difficulty of helping the plight of homeless people as a painful individual moral dilemma, but the difficulty actually comes from failures of the larger institutions on which our common life depends."[38] Because it touches all Americans, institutional failure represents one more link between the underclass and the rest of America—only it impacts poor people with greater force because they lack alternatives. They cannot purchase private schooling, security systems, and health care or, as the well-off have done in central Philadelphia, create their own special service districts to assure clean and safe streets. This cumulative failure of institutions degrades public life and raises the question of whether any common collective life remains possible in American cities. If privatization proves the only viable response, what will prevent the distribution of institutional resources from becoming more unequal? What happens to the definition of citizenship and the possibility of community?[39]

Many institutions have deserted inner cities; the ones that remain are failing; their legitimacy, and the legitimacy of city government itself, has collapsed. Perhaps the most viable institutions remaining in inner cities are churches, which continue to command respect through their secular as well as religious activities. Churches, however, as Gamm points out in his contrast between the impact of Jewish synagogues and Catholic churches in a section of Boston, have contributed to the erosion as well as the stabilization of communities.[40] Attacked for inaccessibility, inadequacy, and unresponsiveness, the institutions that serve inner cities confront in intensified form the crisis of legitimacy that afflicts the public sector and government throughout America.

Institutional withdrawal and collapse not only rob inner cities of the services they need, they knock out the props that sustain a viable public life and the possibility of community. They destroy the basis of "civil society." Denuded of institutions, cities move ineluctably to-

[38] Robert N. Bellah, Richard Madsen, William M. Sullivan, Ann Swidler, and Steven M. Tipton, *The Good Society* (New York: Alfred A. Knopf, 1991), pp. 256, 4.

[39] These are among the questions asked in the excellent book by Jeffrey R. Henig, *Rethinking School Choice: Limits of the Market Metaphor* (Princeton: Princeton University Press, 1994).

[40] This is a major theme of Gamm, "Exodus."

ward privatization and away from a public life, toward anomic individualism and away from community. As community becomes more elusive in inner cities, its restraints and satisfactions disappear, eroding the buffer between individuals and a consumer culture to which they lack access through legitimate means.

Institutional failure, a degraded public life, and the collapse of community do not stop at the borders of inner cities. They diminish the lives of everyone. That is another reason why the problems of the underclass represent in intensified form transformations that are reshaping the rest of America. The renewal of public life and the rebuilding of community require the revitalization of urban institutions. Without a renewed public sphere, no policies directed toward family, work, or welfare will turn around the crisis within America's inner cities.

This view of inner-city poverty as a problem of "place" raises another issue. What are the most promising sites both for research and for the interface between research and public action? University-based research by and large remains trapped within disciplinary boundaries, driven more by the frontiers of disciplines than by the contours and urgency of the issues. Conventional social science expends an inordinate amount of its great energy and talent on devising new ways of answering old questions. Government-driven research asks for answers to the same questions or for evaluations of public policy, not for a new intellectual framework, and by supplying most of the funds, it shapes the agenda of the independent think tanks that dominate poverty research outside of universities. (The Consortium on Chicago School Research provides an outstanding example of a coalition of researchers from universities, not-for-profits, and state and local governments that develops an agenda from current problems and combines research with the dissemination of "usable knowledge." According to its official description, "The Consortium views research not just as a technical operation of gathering data and publishing reports, but as a process of community education advanced through sustained public discourse.")[41]

---

[41] The phrase "usable knowledge" is from Charles E. Lindblom and David K. Cohen, *Usable Knowledge: Social Science and Social Problem Solving* (New Haven: Yale University Press, 1979; the Consortium's statement of purpose may be found on the back cover of

The emergence of an alternative research agenda may require alternative spaces, places where social scientists, organizers, program administrators, political leaders, and community members gather as equals. It requires a disciplined commitment to a combination of research with advocacy and to the popularization of knowledge in a setting in which an urgent commitment to the revitalization of communities rather than to disciplinary rewards drives the direction of research.

Nonetheless, redefining poverty as a problem of "places" rather than "people" raises troublesome questions. Political scientist Margaret Weir, for one, has written the sorry history of "place-based" national antipoverty strategies from 1960 to 1980. In the 1930s, the New Deal confronted poverty with programs directed toward assisting individuals: unemployment and old-age insurance, Social Security, Aid to Dependent Children. Although the War on Poverty extended some of these, notably medical care for the elderly and very poor, place-based policies, centered in the Department of Housing Development, created in 1965, constituted the core of its urban antipoverty strategies. Architects of the antipoverty program turned to place-based policies for two reasons. One was congressional hostility to extending income supports and other forms of social welfare. The other was the dependence of the Democratic Party on urban voters and the dominance of urban interests among congressional Democrats.[42]

For the most part, place-based policies missed their goals. Urban renewal, which predated the War on Poverty, failed to rehouse the low-income people whose homes it tore down. Within cities, politicians and business interests captured a disproportionate share of federal dollars, which they directed toward the rebuilding of downtowns rather the revitalization of neighborhoods. Only through intense mobilization, argues Weir, did representatives of poor people wrest any gains from federal programs. "The struggle for control of

Anthony Bryk, John Q. Easton, David Kerbow, Sharon G. Rollow, and Penny A. Sebring, *A View from the Elementary Schools: The State of Reform in Chicago. A Report of the Steering Committee Consortium on Chicago School Research*, July 1993.

[42] Margaret Weir, "Cities and the Politics of Social Policy in the United States," in Stephan Leibried and Paul Pierson, eds., *Prospects for Social Europe* (forthcoming).

93

these resources," which sometimes succeeded, "often encouraged urban and particularly black political mobilization." As a result, "the War on Poverty and the urban policies that followed it contributed to containing and isolating poverty. . . . The limited resources devoted to the War on Poverty meant that it served far more effectively as a vehicle for black political empowerment than as a remedy for poverty." These place-based policies shared another weakness: they failed to "challenge the growth of political boundaries that had grown up during the 1950s and '60s to divide the metropolitan population by income and race." By acquiescing in the intensification of segregation, they reinforced the increasing poverty of cities and of the people within them. Place-based policies foundered, that is, on the shoals of the suburbs.[43]

Even the limited gains from place-based policies eroded in the conservative years after 1980. As population shifted from city to suburb, political parties depended less on urban votes, and urban interests lost their majority in Congress. In 1980, Ronald Reagan won the presidency without the support of cities. The new Republican strategy stressed lower taxes and the devolution of social responsiblity to states and localities. As a consequence, between 1980 and 1990 the Reagan and Bush administrations slashed grants to cities, according to one estimate, by 46 percent. With the support of Congress, the administration terminated the following programs: the Comprehensive Employment and Training Act, which cities had used as a source of jobs; General Revenue Sharing, which gave cities extra, nontargeted funds; and Urban Development Action Grants, which supported urban redevelopment. At the same time, funds for the construction of public housing nearly ceased. Faced with a shrinking tax base and escalating social problems, such as homelessness, cities could not compensate for the federal dollars they had lost.[44]

Place-based policies, always inadequate, had proved more vulnerable than policies directed toward individuals. Social Security benefits continued to grow with inflation, as did Medicare and Medicaid. The value of Aid to Families with Dependent Children declined by more

[43] Weir, "Cities and the Politics of Social Policy."
[44] Ibid.

than 30 percent, but the program remained largely intact. In American politics, cities remain easier targets than people, and place-based policies have proved a fragile base from which to build a strategy against poverty. Indeed, during the 1980s, Michael J. Rich points out, "the share of federal grants awarded for programs that provide payments to individuals has risen from about one-third to more than one-half, while payments to needy jurisdictions have been terminated or substantially reduced." Community Development Block Grant funding, for instance, dropped by 25 percent during the decade; given inflation, a 1990 CDBG dollar bought only half of what it had a decade earlier. As important as are programs that "focus on education and training, health care, nutrition, alcohol and drug abuse treatment and the like," argues Rich, they do not eliminate the need for "place-oriented programs that attack some of the fundamental causes of poverty, forces manifest in the physical decay of distressed neighborhoods—disinvestment and abandonment of residential and commercial buildings, loss of employment opportunities, aging infrastructure, lack of public facilities such as schools, health clinics, and recreation centers."[45]

New place-based antipoverty strategies differ from the ones deployed in the War on Poverty era. They are local, not national, initiatives. Their funds come from an eclectic collection of sources, not primarily (in many cases, not at all) from the national government. They grow up outside local government; they are not dependent on city governments; their money is relatively safe from capture by politicians and "downtown" interests. Community economic development, the most widespread of the new place-based initiatives, was responsible for most of the low-cost housing built in the 1980s.[46] Diverse and diffuse, other strategies remain, at this writing, difficult to classify and assess. However, across the country, in every city, one finds creative programs for rebuilding and revitalizing communities. Few, however, have enough money for more than small, local successes. Without infusions of funds, their impacts will remain limited. Private resources,

[45] Michael J. Rich, *National Goals and Local Choices: Distributing Federal Aid to the Poor* (Princeton: Princeton University Press, 1993), pp. 345–46.

[46] Mike Davis, "Who Killed LA? Part Two: The Verdict Is Given," *New Left Review* 197 (May-June 1993): 29–54.

even foundations, can do little more than provide seed money or sustain the operating costs of small programs. Only governments can supply the resources needed to rebuild inner cities and improve the lives of their people.

The solution, Rich explains, extends beyond providing funds. The experience of the Community Development Block Grants illustrates that the degree to which federal funds reach the neediest cities and neighborhoods varies widely. A variety of factors have combined, in some instances, to divert federal funds from their intended goals and, in others, to keep them relatively on target. What this implies is the importance of "decision-making systems," patterned interactions between federal, state, and local governments in federal grant-in-aid programs. Despite the many disappointments of the CDBG program, its successes testify both to the crucial role of federal funds in urban regeneration and to the potential of place-based policies.[47]

Caught between declining tax bases, diminished federal funds, and escalating demands for social services, city governments by themselves lack the money with which to fund major initiatives. State governments, dominated by suburban legislators, fund urban programs reluctantly. Even though the legislatures have the formal power to force suburbs to share their resources with cities, the courts, demographic trends, the cumulative impact of public policies, and political realities militate against dismantling the barriers that permit suburbs to hoard their own resources. Only the national government has access to the money for a sustained attack on urban poverty. However, faced with a huge deficit, no longer controlled by urban interests, confronting widespread national hostility to cities, the national government remains an unlikely source for massive new funds, as the lame response to the 1992 civil disorders in Los Angeles illustrates.[48]

Writing in the winter of 1994, I find few grounds for optimism. Only the energy at the grass roots—community development corporations, imaginative social programs, local organizing, dedicated neighbors and volunteers—offer any immediate hope for improving conditions

[47] Rich, *National Goals and Local Choices*, p. 350.

[48] Mike Davis, "Who Killed LA? A Political Autopsy," *New Left Review* 195 (January-February 1993): 3–28.

in America's cities. At least, for the first time in twelve years, a national administration professes concern about the state of the nation's cities and intends to formulate an urban policy, although early proposals suggest means entirely inadequate to the problems. The defeat of President Bill Clinton's modest economic stimulus proposal, with its funds for infrastructure projects in cities, the meager funds allocated to the rebuilding of South Central Los Angeles, the lack of creative urban policy ideas within state and national governments, the resistance of suburbs to sharing revenue or other resources (notably schools), the erosion of urban political power, the economic plight of cities and the escalation of demanding social problems within them, the racial hostility that underlies responses to poverty, the stereotypes of criminal, promiscuous dependence that color images of inner-city populations—together these predict that neither substantial new money nor creative programs will flow toward cities. Even if urban economies improve, prosperity will not reverse the economic restructuring that leaves huge numbers of inner-city residents redundant in the labor market, employable, at best, at poverty wages. Nor, without government forcing suburbs to build massive amounts of low-cost housing, will urban segregation decrease noticeably. As a result, at best, poverty, social isolation, and related problems will stabilize or decline very slightly; at worst, they will increase, accompanied by more books on the shiftless, undeserving, threatening underclass within America's cities.

Underclass, however, is a concept that muddies debate and inhibits the formulation of constructive policy. It reflects the centuries-old preoccupation with dividing poor people into categories of moral worth. As a modern euphemism for the undeserving poor, it reinforces the tradition of blaming the victim. By stigmatizing them, it insults those it designates. It also works against their best interests, for it fosters political divisions among the working class and poor, who need each other as allies, and, through its concentration on the behavior of a relatively small number of people clustered in inner cities, deflects attention from the problem of poverty and minimizes its extent. The word *underclass* has little intellectual substance. It lacks a consistent, defensible theoretical basis. It is not a "class" in any of the usual

97

senses. Most definitions, in fact, as this chapter has argued, substitute varieties of bad behavior for the criteria customary in stratification theories. Nor can social scientists who use it, let alone the media, agree on a definition.

There is a still more fundamental problem with *underclass*. The great transformations concentrating poverty in cities and contributing to the phenomenon labeled *underclass*, which I have discussed in this chapter, are reordering the lives of all Americans by changing their experience of work and family, eroding their once-vital cities, undermining their institutions, and degrading their public life. The problems of the underclass represent in intensified form transformations that are reshaping the rest of America. To talk about the impact of these transformations as if they are confined to one small segment of the population is to miss the point.

Urban Schools

IN NOVEMBER 1989, I was in Chicago for the first major conference sponsored by the Social Science Research Council's Committee for Research on the Urban Underclass. Before going to bed one night, I turned on the late television news in my room in the dingy Holiday Inn near the lake on the city's south side. A local newscaster reported the inauguration of elected councils of parents, community members, and teachers to govern each of the city's nearly six hundred schools. Their election had resulted from a new school-reform law implementing radical decentralization.

Amazed, I wondered, how could this have happened? Why had those of us outside Chicago heard so little about it? Why had the national press paid it so little attention? As a historian of education, I realized immediately that Chicago had undertaken the swiftest, most dramatic structural reform of any urban school system in a century. For years I had argued that most school reform had failed to attack the underlying structures of urban education. I had called for a wholesale attack on bureaucracy and a devolution of control to parents and school sites. There was no inherent reason, I contended, why the structure of schooling should assume classic bureaucratic forms. Even in the late 1960s, I had found myself on the fringe of educational reform. By the 1980s, opponents of community control bandied a twisted version of New York City's experience to discredit the application of local democracy to public schools, and the energies of school reform, channeled by the conservative political culture of the times, pointed in other directions.

I never had expected to see significant control turned over to parents and communities at individual school sites in big cities. In 1989, so futile would the effort have seemed that I would not have bothered to make the arguments in its favor. But it had happened in Chicago. I wanted to know why and, even more, how it worked in practice.

Hardly a detached observer, I wanted to know if the course of school reform would sustain my faith in the capacity of ordinary people to manage their schools and in the liberating effects of shedding bureaucratic weight.

When I returned to the Russell Sage Foundation in New York, my base for the year, and to the University of Pennsylvania, my permanent academic home, I told everyone who would listen about what was happening in Chicago. Few of them knew much about it; very few shared my excitement; most predicted disaster. Here was another surprise. Even among my friends on the political Left, Chicago school reform evoked more skepticism than serious interest. Uneducated parents would prove unable to govern schools; reform was a political ploy that would deliver the schools to machine politics; reform was a stalking horse for vouchers, which would replace public education when reform inevitably failed; decentralization was pointless because no relation exists among school structure, pedagogy, and student achievement. (Even Jonathan Kozol, in his chapter on Chicago's schools in *Savage Inequalities*, dismisses Chicago school reform with a few casual, ill-informed remarks.)[1] How to account for this reflexive negativism became another puzzle. I think it revealed the unease of university-based researchers suddenly declared irrelevant. Chicago school reform had happened without them. If it worked, this reform could undermine professional-driven, expert-led models of educational change and public policy.

Two colleagues at Penn shared my excitement. Michelle Fine, a social psychologist deeply involved with educational reform in Philadelphia, and Elaine Simon, an urban anthropologist and specialist in the qualitative evaluation of educational programs, sensed the pioneering spirit and radical implications of Chicago school reform. Together, we wanted to spend time finding out more about what was happening in the city. Our distinctive contribution, we thought, could be interpreting Chicago school reform for an audience outside the city, promoting its image, countering the negative press it received among those who believed it wouldn't work or who, like teachers' unions or administra-

[1] Jonathan Kozol, *Savage Inequalities: Children in America's Schools* (New York: Crown Publishers, 1991).

tors, saw in it a threat to be avoided at all costs. To finance our exploration of Chicago school reform, we turned to the Spencer Foundation and its president, the late Lawrence Cremin. The dean of American educational historians, Cremin realized the significance of Chicago's experiment, even if he was a bit skeptical about its long-term success. With remarkable speed, he accepted our proposal. His successor, Patricia Graham, also a historian, continued to support our activities, which we have described, only partly facetiously, as a research project without theory, methods, or goal.

Since the spring of 1990, we have poked around Chicago school reform, talking with representatives of all constituencies, attending local school council meetings, visiting schools, reading research reports and newspaper articles. Although we share an interpretation of Chicago school reform, each of us thinks from the standpoint of our own special training and perspectives about the way reform resonates. In my case, it's history. As it does with welfare and the "underclass," history proves essential for interpreting the meaning and prospects of school reform. Indeed, American public education remains conditioned by its nineteenth-century origins. Explanations of public education's structure, ideological underpinnings, social role, or the dynamics of reform begin in the past. Here, I want to identify the impulses underlying the origins of public education, which, as with welfare reform or approaches to urban poverty, partly have been about improving poor people. Having set the stage, I want to show how Chicago school reform simultaneously resonates with and transcends the history of education. The story is instructive for thinking about education's future as well as its past.

THE ORIGINS OF PUBLIC EDUCATION

The emergence of systems of public education constitutes the core of the story. The word *systems* is crucial because schools existed before the nineteenth century, and usually they received some support from public funds, although the line separating public and private lacked even the rough precision it acquired later in the century. In cities, by the latter-nineteenth century, the haphazard collection of schools dotted about town and country had been transformed into educational systems: articulated, age-graded, hierarchically structured groupings of schools, primarily free and often compulsory, administered by full-time experts and increasingly taught by specially trained staff.[2] What accounts for the sudden development of a new social institution destined to define the childhood and adolescent experience of nearly all Americans?

Systems of public education originated as responses to major problems worrying many nineteenth-century Americans, and they coincided with crucial developments that reshaped American society during the first three-quarters of the nineteenth century. In retrospect, the fit between systems of public education and massive economic and social transformation appears almost too tidy. How could the outcome have been otherwise? Is this not a story of how inevitable change occurred? The answer is no. As chapter 1 pointed out, in the early- and mid-nineteenth century, architects of major social institutions debated alternative models, which differed from one another on a number of dimensions: source of control, scale, finance, and professionalism. Examples of each—paternalistic voluntarism, corporate voluntarism, democratic localism, and incipient bureaucracy—existed, championed by promoters as the appropriate template for the future of public schooling. Not merely technical, the debates reflected differences in social values, in the priorities with which people of the time confronted the changes engulfing their towns and cities. In public education, the model that won was bureaucracy, and we live with it still. But we should remember that it was not the only available alternative nor, as the Chicago experience discussed below illustrates, the only one possible in a complex, advanced society.

Localism did not give way entirely to state bureaucracy. Despite state regulation, individual towns and cities retained significant control of the financing and content of public schooling. As a result, spending on public schools, dependent on a combination of property tax base and local commitment to education, varied widely among

[2] The discussion of the origins of public education that follows draws on the essays in my book *Reconstructing American Education* (Cambridge: Harvard University Press, 1987), where full documentation may be found.

neighboring towns and cities within the same state. In the nineteenth and early-twentieth centuries, large cities generally afforded and built advanced educational facilities, which, although demanded and used most by affluent families, remained available to working-class children as well. With income variation and ethnic segregation less pronounced than they are today, public schools served, albeit imperfectly, as sites in which youngsters of different backgrounds mingled with one another. The first major break in this approximation of urban common schooling came in the nineteenth century with the creation of specialized schools attended, disproportionately, by children of different class backgrounds; the gap widened in the early-twentieth century with the introduction of tracking, especially in high schools, which separated students by aspiration and achievement, often highly correlated with class and ethnicity. After World War II, a new urban ecology reversed the existing urban economic balance by shifting resources away from cities and into suburbs, thereby heightening disparities in educational opportunities. Because most African Americans remained in or migrated to cities, the new urban ecology also heightened segregation, which, as chapter 2 observed, reinforced both poverty and educational inequity. Attempts to overcome the historic localism of public education by forcing suburbs to share educational resources with cities foundered in the Supreme Court, notably in 1974 in *Milliken v. Bradley*. By the late-twentieth century, therefore, the social ecology of public education mocked the common-school ideal that underlay the origins of public school systems in the nineteenth century.[3]

The origins of public educational systems in cities and large towns coincided with rapid urbanization, industrialization, immigration, and the emergence of a working, or wage-labor, class. A massive increase in both crime and poverty, argued many nineteenth-century observers, accompanied this social and economic transformation. One response, as chapter 1 showed, was the reorganization of poor

[3] Ira Katznelson and Margaret Weir, *Schooling for All: Class, Race, and the Decline of the Democratic Ideal* (New York: Basic Books, 1985); Harvey Kantor and Barbara Brenzel, "Urban Education and the 'Truly Disadvantaged': The Historical Roots of the Contemporary Crisis, 1945–1960," in Michael B. Katz, ed., *The "Underclass" Debate: Views from History* (Princeton: Princeton University Press, 1993).

relief and the introduction of poorhouses. Another was the creation of public schools. As with ideas about poverty, educational thought translated crime and poverty into moral problems. Lower-class urban families, who failed to implant earnestness and restraint in the character of their children, were breeding grounds for paupers and criminals. Public education would offer an alternative environment and a first-rate set of adult models, a cheap and superior substitute for the jail and the poorhouse. Although their cost might seem high, schools in the long run would decrease the financial burden of adult crime and poverty.

With the mid-nineteenth-century arrival of massive numbers of famine Irish, the ethnic composition of expanding cities became a source of special anxiety for many people who equated cultural diversity with immorality and deviance. To respectable Americans, poor Irish Catholics appeared alien, uncouth, and menacing. Here, as with crime, education assumed a crucial role. Although the personalities and behavior of adult immigrants might prove intractable, the pending rot of Anglo-American Protestant civilization could be averted through a concerted effort to shape the pliable characters of their children into a native mold. As the key instruments in the massive task of assimilation, schools undertook the transformation of immigrant children into Americans. In a literal sense, public education often has been about improving poor people. In 1858, the Boston School Committee described its task as "taking children at random from a great city, undisciplined, uninstructed, often with inveterate forwardness and obstinacy, and with the inherited stupidity of centuries of ignorant ancestors; transforming them from animals into intellectual beings; giving to many their first appreciation of what is wise, what is true, what is lovely, and what is pure."[4] Subsequent events—the late-nineteenth- and early-twentieth-century immigration from southern and eastern Europe—only strengthened the role of schools as agents of cultural standardization. Confronted with the new immigration in contemporary America, opponents of bilingual education would have schools continue their historic role today.

Nothing more sharply differentiated the experiences of black Amer-

[4] Boston School Committee, *Annual Report*, 1858, p. 10–11.

icans from immigrants than the role of schooling. Ira Katznelson and Margaret Weir point to the "commitment to educate all children in primary schools paid for by the government" as "the most distinctive American public policy of the early nineteenth century."[5] Nonetheless, it was a policy for white Americans only. In the antebellum South, state laws forbade teaching slaves to read and write. In the North, even as school promoters championed the embrace of immigrants in common schools, where they would mix with and become Americans, they supported segregated schools for blacks. Even when northern state laws abolished segregation in the latter-nineteenth century, cities devised school boundaries in ways that kept blacks largely segregated. In the twentieth century, as northern legislatures abolished segregation and courts ruled against real-estate practices that preserved the racial exclusiveness of city neighborhoods, suburbanization offered white Americans a legal way to keep themselves and their children separate from blacks.

The fear of crime and immigration that propelled the origins of public educational systems rested more on perception than fact, more on evasive stereotypes than on confrontion with the structural sources of anxiety. Crime, it appears, was much less of a problem than people imagined; increasing expenses for poor relief resulted from the transformation of work and the ecology of cities (discussed in chapters 1 and 2); immigrants, research now argues, represented a select, highly motivated, and unusually literate sector of Irish society. They were not intemperate, shiftless, and ignorant, as nativists portrayed them. Fear and distrust of cultural diversity ran deep in nineteenth-century America. Whatever its sources, it proved a powerful political and social force cementing nativism to public schooling with a bond that has held for 150 years and shows no sign of weakening. The displacement of the responsibility for preventing crime and reducing pauperism onto the schools also remained fixed as a feature of social policy. Schooling became a cheap and easy substitute for direct, uncomfortable confrontation with the nasty, intractable sources of social problems.

School promoters also expected public education to alleviate some

[5] Katnelson and Weir, *Schooling for All*, pp. 9–10.

of the strains associated with the emergence of capitalism. Although the pace of change varied from region to region and stages overlapped, the most important development in the late-eighteenth and early-nineteenth centuries was not industry or urbanism but the spread of capitalism, by which I mean, following Dobb, not solely a market system but the transformation of labor into a commodity "bought and sold on the market like any other object of exchange."[6] Its hallmark was the spread of wage labor. To take a striking example, according to Carl Kaestle, the proportion of men listing themselves simply as laborer increased between 1796 and 1855 from 5.5 percent to 27.4 percent.[7] Older forms of apprenticeship, which rested on bound labor, virtually disappeared during the same years. Other historians have pointed to an upsurge in the wandering poor starting in the late-eighteenth century and to extraordinary working-class population mobility in the mid-nineteenth. Still others have documented the abandonment of mercantilism by state governments. My own research offers empirical demonstration of the bifurcation of the social structure of two nineteenth-century cities into a working and business class and the formation of a large, permanent group of wage workers.[8] Historians using primarily nonquantitative data also have documented the emergence of a working class and highlighted its ideological and political significance.[9]

The diffusion of wage labor as a template for social as well as economic relations stands out as crucial to the story of institutional creation. The temporal association, in fact, is very clear because early institutional development, including the emergence of public school systems, bears a closer relationship to capitalism than to industrializa-

[6] Maurice Dobb, *Studies in the Development of Capitalism*, rev. ed. (New York: International Publishers, 1963), p. 7.

[7] Carl F. Kaestle, *The Evolution of an Urban School System: New York City, 1750–1850* (Cambridge: Harvard University Press, 1974), p. 102.

[8] For an empirical account of social structure, see Michael B. Katz, Mark J. Stern, and Michael J. Doucet, *The Social Organization of Early Industrial Capitalism* (Cambridge: Harvard University Press, 1982).

[9] As examples, see Sean Wilentz, *Chants Democratic: New York City and the Rise of the American Working Class, 1788–1850* (New York: Oxford University Press, 1984); and Bruce Laurie, *Working People of Philadelphia, 1800–1850* (Philadelphia: Temple University Press, 1980).

tion, whose takeoff dates primarily from the 1840s. As chapter 1 showed, dissatisfaction in New York State with the existing system of poor relief led to the passage of the law creating specialized county poorhouses in 1825; the first special institution for juvenile vagrants and delinquents opened in 1827; the New York Public School Society emerged out of the Free School Society in 1824. In Massachusettts the first state hospital for the mentally ill opened in 1833; poor relief underwent fundamental shifts in the 1820s; agitation for educational reform began in the same decade.

Institutions reflected the drive toward order, rationality, discipline, and specialization inherent in capitalism. There is a parallel between the way a capitalist society processes its business and the way it processes its problems. One problem, work discipline, which observers report in developing societies today, arose first in its modern form during the emergence of capitalism in Britain, as E. P. Thompson has described.[10] It reflected the tension between customary rhythms of life and the requirements of urban and industrial work settings and the contrast between ascriptive and achievement-based systems of reward. In contrast to the punctuality, regularity, docility, and deferral of gratification demanded in a modern workforce, both peasant and urban populations usually had governed their activities more by the sun than by the clock, more by the season and customary festivities than by externally imposed production schedules. And it was correct, not corrupt, to favor a kinsman or fellow villager over a more qualified stranger in the award of jobs or favors.

Schools assumed major responsibility for transforming these patterns of work and reward into steady, punctual, time-driven labor rewarded, in theory, by merit. Equality of educational opportunity and professionalization, which became goals of education in the nineteenth century, encouraged the substitution of achievement for ascription as the basis of rewards and employment. State authorities complained repeatedly about local school committees that hired teachers on the basis of friendship or kinship rather than merit, experience, or professional qualaifications. Everywhere, in reports of local school

[10] E. P. Thompson, "Time, Work Discipline, and Industrial Capitalism," *Past and Present* 38 (1967): 56–97.

committees, the major obsessions—and difficulties—were punctuality and regularity of attendance, while the villains were parents uneducated in the importance of schooling who allowed or encouraged their children to remain at home for what, to school promoters, appeared whimsical reasons or who took the side of their child against the teacher. The mass production of clocks and watches began at about the same time as the mass production of public schools.

Besides prompting the need to train and discipline an increasingly urban workforce, early American capitalism influenced the development of public education through its association with democracy, that is, through the links between class formation and political structure. Unlike their European counterparts, white male American workers did not have to struggle for the franchise. Consequently, they viewed the state as a potential if not immediate ally and channeled their protests through votes and the political process rather than through direct action. "Mass common schooling under public auspices," Ira Katznelson and Margaret Weir point out, developed in antebellum America in part because "working people . . . joined a coalition favoring such schools while at the same time many of their counterparts in Europe were resisting state schooling because unlike European workers, white male working-class Americans were voting citizens."[11]

Antebellum workers did not resist the idea of public education; they protested developments they thought rendered it less democratic or useful for their childen. In the 1830s and 1840s, for instance, democratic ideology influenced successful attacks on the monitorial system that had dominated urban schooling for two or three decades. The monitorial system was associated with both the devolution of responsiblity for popular education to private assocations and a dual structure of education in which "public," as in "public education," signified "pauper," because public education was free. The first generation of common school reformers, represented by Horace Mann and Henry Barnard, transformed the meaning of public education by breaking this association between public and pauper. Democratic ideas also underlay early attacks on state government attempts to centralize education by establishing boards of education and normal schools,

[11] Katznelson and Weir, *Schooling for All*, p. 9.

which some critics feared as the first step in the imposition of state ideology. Working-class representatives also sometimes protested the introduction of high schools, which, they argued, delivered their tax money to the wealthy, whose children were the only ones who could afford to use them.

Urbanism, the spread of wage labor, and technological change fostered another new problem—idle youth—that many people at the time tried to solve through the expansion of schooling. Moralism aside, contemporary complaints about idle and vagrant youths roaming the streets of towns and cities reflected actual social behavior; observers saw in nineteenth-century cities a genuine crisis of youth. In earlier times, long-standing customs had defined the expectations and duties of people throughout their life course. Young people had left home, perhaps around the age of fourteen, to work as servants or apprentices, almost always dwelling in another household. Never had it been unclear where youngsters should live or how they should spend their time. Idleness was unimaginable.

In the late-eighteenth and early-nineteenth centuries, the numbers of young people in towns and cities increased enormously while the institution of apprenticeship decayed. The practice of keeping male servants had nearly disappeared even earlier. Whether opportunities for domestic service for young women decreased is unknown, but large numbers were neither at work for wages nor in school.

These customary ways of spending the years between puberty and marriage began to disappear before the creation of an institutional network to replace them by containing and managing young people, who now, often, literally had nothing to do. Indeed, in the era of commercial capitalism, before industrialization, little work existed for young men in commercial cities. Without schools or jobs, large numbers remained idle until young men became old enough to find work and young women married. High schools developed during this crisis of youth partly to provide a safe and constructive setting for young people. In the places I have studied, the establishment of a school system with special provisions for young people over the age of eleven or twelve quickly and dramatically reduced the proportion of idle youth. Many youngsters entered school simply because they could not find work. When factory jobs first became available, large numbers of working-class young men left the schools while their more affluent contemporaries—and young women—remained behind.

Parents worried about more than the idleness of their children. Within nineteenth-century cities, sharply entrenched patterns of inequality coexisted with massive, rapid population turnover. Fathers usually passed on their status to their children, but rates of short-term social mobility remained very high and businessmen failed with extraordinary frequency. At the same time, technological development rendered the position of artisans increasingly insecure by severing the link between skill and reward that had formed the hallmark of many crafts. With downward mobility frequent, with craftsmen unable to pass on valuable skills to their sons, many parents hoped schooling would help secure their children's future. How, then, should children spend their adolescent years? Fierce debates between supporters of public high schools and residential academies reflected the pervasive anxiety and unease about adolescence at the time. No school, opponents of residential academies argued, could replicate a family, and, with domesticity an increasing cultural value, a family environment seemed more and more crucial. Despite a good deal of egalitarian rhetoric about equality of educational opportunity, I suspect that parental anxiety about their adolescent children, especially in moderately affluent families who otherwise would have strained to pay tuition at private schools, fueled the creation of public secondary schools and solidified the commitment of the middle classes to public education.

Notice a missing goal among the original purposes of public education: the cultivation and transmission of cognitive skills and intellectual abilities as ends in themselves. Public school systems existed to shape behavior and attitudes, alleviate social and family problems, and to improve poor people and reinforce a social structure under stress. The character of pupils assumed much more importance than their minds.

Public school promoters talked less about gender than about crime and poverty, cultural diversity, the need to train and discipline an urban workforce, the problem of idle youth, or anxieties about adolescence and families. Most (though by no means all) of the early writing on public education was by men, and men held the key legislative and administrative positions. Nonetheless, the origins of public school systems affected women profoundly. For one thing, public schools opened new, more extensive educational opportunities to them. The ease and speed with which public schools became coeducational, as David Tyack and Elizabeth Hansot show, remains one of the most intriguing stories in American educational history.[12] In fact, women soon made disproportionate use of public schools, remaining in school longer than men and dominating early high schools. The attraction of prolonged schooling for young women rested partly in its association with teaching, the first semiprofessional occupation largely available to women.[13] Between the early- and mid-nineteenth century, in most parts of the United States, teaching, especially the teaching of young children, feminized. Women teachers offered two advantages: they appeared uniquely suited to the education of young children and they were paid half as much as men. Indeed, an oversupply of cheap female labor permitted the expansion and extension of public schooling.

Nineteenth-century educational promoters not only erected school systems; they also helped engineer a lasting popular conversion to public education as both the cornerstone of democracy and the key agency for the solution of virtually every major social problem. Their success reflected the resonance of the American theory of public education with the premises of democratic capitalism in the same era. It reflected, too, the usefulness of public education for displacing social problems and avoiding redistributive reform. In both their strengths and their limits, school systems, with their emphasis on equal access and unequal rewards, their sometimes fictive meritocracy, and their bureaucratic organization of experience, became miniature versions of America's social and political order.[14]

[12] David Tyack and Elizabeth Hansot, *Learning Together: A History of Coeducation in American Schools* (New Haven: Yale University Press; New York: Russell Sage Foundation, 1990).

[13] Maris A. Vinovskis, "The Female School Teacher in Ante-Bellum Massachusetts," *Journal of Social History* 10 (1977): 332–45.

[14] The issue of meritocracy in American educational history is complicated. David F. Labaree, *The Making of an American High School: The Credentials Market and Central High of Philadelphia, 1838–1939* (New Haven: Yale University Press, 1988) shows that al-

CHICAGO SCHOOL REFORM AS HISTORY

Once set in place, the organization of early public school systems channeled the subsequent history of urban education along bureaucratic grooves that constrained the possibility of far-reaching structural reform. Almost without realizing the historic significance of its actions, in October 1989, Chicago began a process of school reform that transcends these historic constraints on change imposed by the origins of urban school systems. Nonetheless, despite its originality, Chicago school reform resonates with the origins of public education and with most of the great themes that have shaped urban school systems and the struggles surrounding them for 150 years. Understanding Chicago school reform's place in history clarifies both its significance for the challenges before it and for the theory and practice of American urban education. Here, I discuss the relations between Chicago school reform and history around five topics: (1) the origins of bureaucracy and the ascendance of experts and professionals; (2) educational reform as a social movement; (3) race and ethnicity, or schools as contested terrain; (4) the revitalization of the public sphere; and (5) the limits of educational reform. I then turn to the implications of these historical resonances for thinking about the dilemmas and obstacles confronting this extraordinary and exciting adventure in school reform.

Chicago school reform refers to a legislative act, a process, and a social movement. As a legislative act, it signifies the radical decentralization of the city's school system achieved through the passage of the Chicago School Reform Act (P.A. 85-1418) by the Illinois legislature on December 2, 1988. As a process, it refers to an ongoing attempt to implement both the letter and spirit of the act, that is, to change both the structure and content of public schooling through the transformation of educational governance. As a social movement, Chicago school reform means the mobilization of communities around the cause of edu-

---

though the social composition of Philadelphia's Central High School in the nineteenth and early-twentieth centuries was strongly biased toward the middle classes, within the school class had little, if any, influence on educational achievement.

cational reform, the democratization of relations in school governance, and the revitalization of the public sphere. This chapter uses *Chicago school reform* in each of these three senses.

To begin, a word about Chicago school reform as a legislative act. Under the Chicago School Reform Act, voters elect a Local School Council (LSC) for each of the city's nearly six hundred schools. Six parents, two community members, two teachers, the principal, and, in high schools, a student (originally as nonvoting, now voting except on personnel issues) member formed each Council. Councils hire principals, now stripped of tenure and placed on four-year contracts. Certification requirements for principals have been liberalized. Principals choose teachers for their schools and fire unsatisfactory ones with less difficulty than before. Councils have broad authority over curriculum and school management, and they control a sizable amount of state money previously routed through the central bureaucracy. A decision of the Illinois Supreme Court in November 1990 declared the initial method of electing LSC members unconstitutional because it violated the principle of one-person, one-vote. As a result, the legislature developed a modified election procedure for the second set of LSC elections, held in November 1991. School reform legislation also capped expenses for administration. Together with the loss of funds now passed directly to schools, the ceiling on administrative costs forced the central office to downsize by laying off hundreds of staff members. Whole wings of the massive former factory on Pershing Road that houses the system's central administration now lie empty.

One of the architects of Chicago school reform, Michael Bakalis, told two of its historians, "Every group you talk to will claim they were the prime movers behind school reform."[15] My colleagues and I can confirm his prediction; everyone we interviewed told us a slightly different story about the origins and early experience of school reform. None of them was wrong; their stories reflected their own part in the process, the corner they occupied, the angle from which they looked out at unfolding events. Chicago school reform happened because of the efforts of an extraordinary, diverse, multiracial, cross-class coali-

[15] Charles L. Kyle and Edward R. Kantowicz, *Kids First—Primero Los Niños: Chicago School Reform in the 1980s* (Springfield, Ill.: Sangamon State University, 1992), p. 7.

tion. One of the most fascinating stories in the history of American education, the account of its orgins also is one of the most intricate and multilayered. It has been told well elsewhere, and I will not repeat it in detail here.[16] However, even a rudimentary overview of its origins helps with the interpretation of Chicago school reform.

As educational reform became a national issue in the 1980s, evidence of failure in Chicago's public schools had begun to mount. Already, the school system had been attacked both by groups within the city and elsewhere, including the federal government, for its intransigent refusal to implement a desegregation plan. After years of resistance, the city entered into a consent decree with the Department of Health, Education, and Welfare in 1980; in 1983, a Monitoring Commission to watch over the implementation of the decree was established, although by then, in a system with 15 percent white students, 19 percent Latino, and over 60 percent black, real desegregation had become impossible.

In addition to the desegregation Monitoring Commission, the imposition of another monitoring body had removed significant authority from the city's school board. As a result largely of fiscal mismanagement, in 1979 the school system teetered on the edge of bankruptcy. With the 1975–76 fiscal crisis of New York City in mind, the Illinois government, as part of its bailout, mandated the creation of a School Finance Authority with significant powers of financial oversight and control. Thus, by the late 1970s, the school system appeared unable to meet its legal or financial obligations without outside supervision, even though its administration had swollen. In the early 1980s, the public schools employed about 4,500 administrators while, according to one report, the city's Catholic schools, with about 42,000 students,

[16] For excellent discussions of the history of the legislation and the early experience of the reform see G. Alfred Hess Jr., *School Restructuring, Chicago Style* (Newbury Park, Calif.: Corwin Press, 1991); Mary O'Connell, *School Reform Chicago Style: How Citizens Organized to Change Public Policy*, a special issue of *The Neighborhood Works* (Chicago: Center for Neighborhood Technology, spring 1991); Kyle and Kantowicz, *Kids First*; and David Moberg, "Can Democracy Save Chicago's Schools?" *American Prospect* 8 (winter 1992): 98–108. For ongoing information about Chicago school reform see *Catalyst: Voices of Chicago School Reform*, Linda Lenz, editor, a publication of the Community Renewal Society, 332 South Michigan Avenue, Chicago, Illinois 60604. The following account is based on Kyle and Kantowicz, *Kids First*; Hess, *School Restructuring*; and O'Connell, *School Reform*; as well as on our interviews and observations.

managed with a total of 32 professionals and about 10 clerical workers in the central office.[17]

In 1985, three reports on dropouts highlighted the system's educational failure. In two high schools, according to the first report, the dropout rate was 70 percent. The school administration intensified its own problems by first trying to discredit the reports and then issuing its own sets of conflicting statistics, each one showing a different dropout rate, all calculated in ways that minimized the problem. In the same year, the Illinois legislature passed a school reform bill that, among other provisions, required school districts to issue an annual report card detailing achievement for each school. Chicago's first report card underlined the dismal situation in the schools. Almost all the city's schools ranked low both within the state and on national measures. President Ronald Reagan's secretary of education, William Bennett, fueled the growing criticism in November 1987 when, on a trip to Chicago, he declared the city's schools the worst in the nation.

Around the city individuals and organizations not affiliated with the school system drew together to advance school reform. Partly through the organizing work of Saul Alinsky as well as from the legacy of the Civil Rights Movement and the War on Poverty, Chicago reformers found support in an unusually vibrant and extensive infrastructure of advocacy organizations. Tensions between blacks, Latinos, and whites, as well as conflicts within the black and Latino communities, hampered early attempts to link them together in a citywide coalition. Indeed, they have continued to fuel tensions within the reform process. Nonetheless, a remarkably diverse coalition gradually emerged, led by the 1985 establishment of CURE (Chicagoans United to Reform Education).

. . . . .

We were scheduled to leave from our first visit to Chicago around noon on a Saturday. One of the people we interviewed told us that the Citywide Coalition for School Reform was meeting early Saturday morning at the offices of the Chicago Urban League on the city's south side. He telephoned the Coalition's executive, who said we were welcome to attend. Not sure of

[17] Kyle and Kantowicz, *Kids First*, p. 169.

what the Coalition was, but with nothing else planned, we decided to spend a couple of hours at the meeting on our way to the airport.

Originally sponsored by Leadership for Quality Education, the educational reform arm of the business community, the Coalition brought together representatives of nearly all the organized groups involved in one way or another with reform. Although it produced some films about school reform, the Coalition served primarily as a friendly forum in which to share problems and debate issues.

Walking into the meeting a few minutes after it had started, we were startled by the group's diversity. Nowhere had we encountered an organization so representative of a city's population. Black, Latino, and Hispanic; from the professions and the working class; men and women in their twenties through their seventies; teachers and school critics; lawyers, accountants, and the representatives of media who offered their services to reform; foundation officials and representatives of business. Their commitment to reform electrified the room. They did not agree with one another on every issue, but their disagreements grew out of a shared belief in the importance and principles of reform.

We were fortunate to receive invitations to subsequent school reform retreats sponsored by the Coalition. At each of them, roughly the same diverse members assembled. We marveled at their energy, their ability to sustain a high level of commitment, and the time they devoted to reform. Despite hearing sharp disagreements on issues, we sensed no wavering of belief in the fundamentals of reform or commitment to its advance. We left each gathering of the Coalition high on the possibilities of democracy, worried about specific problems encountered by reform, but optimistic about its hold on the city.

· · · · ·

Chicago school reformers drew on two crucial advantages: a coherent plan and money. Designs for Change, a research and advocacy organization led by Don Moore, supplied research, theory, and practical strategies for implementing reform. Other organizations, notably the Chicago Panel on Public School Policy and Finance, led by Fred Hess, also contributed research and ideas. As a result, Chicago school reform rested on both an unusually detailed and solid body of

116

empirical evidence and a carefully articulated theory of school improvement that emphasized the relation between educational change and governance.

Chicago's business community supplied both money and influence to support reform. A 1981 study showing massive mismanagement in the schools had alarmed and aroused business leaders; they lost even more faith when in 1987 the superintendent, Manford Byrd, solicited their cooperation in a plan to guarantee jobs for high school graduates but refused to guarantee improvement in school outcomes. Business leaders also found themselves increasingly dissatisfied with the products of the city's public schools and worried about filling their future employment needs. As a result, they supported the work of Designs for Change and other reform groups and paid for the massive lobbying effort that steered school reform through the Illinois legislature.

Although Mayor Harold Washington, elected in 1983, adopted school reform as a key objective, his first school "summit" in 1986–87 failed. Events, however, soon drew him into school reform again. On September 8, 1987, the teachers struck the city schools for the ninth time in seventeen years. The nineteen-day strike, the longest in the city's history, fueled demands for reform by intensifying criticism of the schools, teachers, and Pershing Road (the administration). Following the strike, Washington assembled another summit and appointed a fifty-member parent/community council to hold meetings and sustain enthusiasm for reform throughout the city. Shortly afterward, on Thanksgiving Day 1987, Washington died of a massive heart attack. Observers offer different interpretations of the impact of his death on reform. Some believe that Washington would not have allowed reform to follow so radical a course, especially one that stripped hundreds of middle-class blacks of their jobs in the school system. Others think the arguments for radical school reform would have convinced him to support the plans advanced by leading reformers. For many of his associates, the continuation of the summit and the success of school reform became a memorial to Washington's efforts.

Nonetheless, the summit, hampered by a lack of leadership from acting mayor Eugene Sawyer, proved slower than CURE to develop plans. According to Kyle and Kantowicz, the "education summit, and

117

particularly its leading edge, the parent/community council, performed a valuable service by channeling and focusing public outrage" after the 1987 teachers' strike. "They kept the momentum of the teachers' strike alive and ensured that some reform bill would pass in 1988."[18] They failed to shape the legislation in any but minor ways, however.

In early 1988, a new, more inclusive coalition of reformers, ABCs (Alliance for Better Chicago Schools) succeeded CURE. Even the powerful teachers' union decided to support reform, although with some misgivings, and to throw its weight behind the passage of a school reform bill. Only the principals' union remained opposed. "The winning alliance that gathered its forces in the winter of 1987–88," observe Kyle and Kantowicz, "bridged the sharp ethnic and racial divisions of the city and reached across class lines, from ghetto streets to corporate boardrooms."[19] With continued support from the business community and the city's foundations (organized into the Donors Forum), reformers took their proposals to the legislature in the session that began in June 1988. Leaving nothing to chance, they mounted a brilliant campaign, employing lobbyists, ferrying busloads of parents to the state capitol in Springfield, working behind the scenes with leading legislators. In December 1988, after a tense six months that included the governor's veto of one bill, the legislature voted school reform into law. The legislature had launched a process that challenged the intellectual and organizational foundations of urban public education.

*The Origins of Bureaucracy and the Ascendance of
Experts and Professionals*

Chicago school reform reinforces historic and theoretical arguments rejecting the contemporary notion that highly centralized, hierarchical, bureaucratic structures are inevitable and inescapable. Whether in the public or private sphere, rigid, hierarchical bureaucracies now have few defenders. The problem has been finding alternative models because throughout the twentieth century, social theorists have found

[18] Ibid., p. 246.
[19] Ibid., p. 225.

118

bureaucracy uniquely appropriate to modern industrial societies. Its rule-driven division of labor, elaborate classifications, and centralized authority all have appeared inescapable prerequisites for accomplishing complicated tasks quickly, predictably, and efficiently on a large scale.

For these reasons, the architects of public school systems believed in bureaucracy, although they did not use the term. Indeed, especially in the third quarter of the nineteenth century, urban schoolmen pioneered in the creation of public bureaucracies. Faced with the task of translating common school ideals of free, universal schooling into practice in burgeoning, diverse cities, they drew on manufacturing and military analogies to erect the first urban school systems. At first they lacked a master plan, but step-by-step the earliest big-city superintendents solved problems of classification, supervision, and coordination by age grading, differentiating levels of schooling, introducing new layers of administrators, defining criteria for employment, improving job security, building career ladders, and centralizing curricula. They justified their decisions on grounds of efficiency, economy, and expertise. They saw, in fact, no viable alternatives.[20]

Others, however, did. The history of public education in the first half of the nineteenth century, as I have observed earlier, reflects a struggle among alternative models of organization: paternalistic voluntarism, corporate voluntarism, democratic localism, and incipient bureaucracy. They differed not only on details but in their position on important dimensions of organization: scale, finance, professionalism, and control. They varied, too, in the social values or priorities on which they rested, the importance they placed on community and democracy, or efficiency and economy. In the end, bureaucracy triumphed. Bureaucracy served the aspirations and convenience of schoolmen far better than the needs of children and their families, and they defended it for more than a century as not only appropriate but inescapable. Now, by demonstrating an alternative model, which emphasizes community, democracy, and flexibility, the process of Chi-

[20] This interpretation of the origins of bureaucracy and of alternative models of organization (see the next paragraph) is based on my analysis in *Reconstructing American Education.*

119

cago school reform is exposing as wrong the assumption that highly centralized bureaucracies are inescapable. Even within a great post-industrial city, the possible modes of organizing schools mock the constricted vision that has trapped the organization of public education within narrow, bureaucratic forms for so long.

By rejecting conventional bureaucratic models of organization, the implementation of Chicago school reform challenges historic processes of professionalization and the ascendance of experts. School administration, like several other professions new in the nineteenth century, emerged out of institutional practice. Lacking precedents and models, the first superintendents created their role. As enough of them appeared around the country, they began to meet regularly, form new associations, share common problems, and try to heighten their influence on local educational policy.[21] Tipping the balance of power between communities and professionals in their own favor ranked high among their concerns. Professionalism meant distancing decisions about policy and the day-to-day operation of schools from parents as well as from politicians and, even, from school boards. To a remarkable degree, late-nineteenth- and early-twentieth-century urban schoolmen successfully insulated their systems from outside influence, fending off or deflecting periodic attacks, reshaping innovations to fit existing structures, and erecting immense self-protective, self-justifying machines held together by mutual self-interest.

Universities combined with the new social and behavioral sciences to abet the process of professionalization. Responding first to the need for massive numbers of high school teachers, universities created departments of education in the late-nineteenth century; most of these became schools of education in the third decade of the twentieth century. Just as school systems sought autonomy from their communities, education professors wanted independence within universities. Like school systems, schools of education became increasingly insular, self-contained, self-protective worlds in minimal contact with their university communities. Schools of education took their lead from the

[21] On the history of educational administration as a field, see David Tyack and Elizabeth Hansot, *Managers of Virtue: Public School Leadership in America, 1820–1980* (New York: Basic Books, 1982).

increasingly elaborate occupational division of labor within school systems to create programs tailored to the new specialties. Their research justified and refined methods of sorting, testing, and tracking. School systems hired their senior faculty to conduct comprehensive surveys. Tapping their networks of former students, influential faculty shaped the senior administration of school systems.

The symbiotic relationship joining these university-based educational barons and practicing administrators reinforced the resistance of school systems to outside pressure and their resilient capacity to absorb innovations without change.[22] Professionalism and expertise became (as they did in other areas of practice and social science) ideologies rooted only partly in accomplishment, serving occupational needs, and legitimated by pretensions to an "objectivity" belied by the influence of a host of contextual factors. The ability to deliver played only a minimal role in the social construction of some new professions. As a result, in education, by the late-nineteenth century, outsiders had begun to criticize the size and cost of school systems as well as their failure to deliver quality education. Nonetheless, the coalition of school professionals and academic experts first formed in the nineteenth century acquired both symbolic and political power, for its growth facilitated and legitimated the divorce of school from community and the subordination of parents to professionals.

Therefore, the concept and process of Chicago school reform assaults the foundations of intellectual authority in schooling as well as customary patterns of control. This is why it arouses so much resistance not only among teachers but also among many university-based researchers. Teachers' skepticism and caution reflect sound instincts, for they have usually played an ambiguous role in school reform. Although reformers have criticized teachers harshly, they have expected them to tranform their practice, either by themselves, with guidance from outsiders, or under pressure from laypersons lacking professional knowledge and skill. Reform, in fact, frequently places tremen-

---

[22] Michael B. Katz, "From Theory to Survey in Graduate Schools of Education," *Journal of Higher Education* 37 (June 1966): 325–34; Arthur G. Powell, *The Uncertain Profession: Harvard and the Search for Educational Authority* (Cambridge: Harvard University Press, 1980).

dous burdens on teachers, whose effective workload expands with no compensating increase in authority or pay. Indeed, Lawrence Cremin wrote that progressive education failed in part because of the excessive demands it placed on teachers.[23]

Tensions between reformers and teachers or administrators are not new. School systems have proved remarkably adept at absorbing, reshaping, and denaturing innovation. When threatened with what they cannot resist, their response more often than not has been mimetic, a shadow reform of features without substance. In the late-nineteenth century, to take one example, early kindergartens, with a social-reform thrust directed to young children from poor families, arose outside school systems. Their advocates intended them to operate in ways and with purposes distinct from public schools. When forced to incorporate kindergartens, public schools kept the name but dropped the differences; kindergartens became preparation for grade one.[24] This history of the kindergarten shows how the intersection of bureaucratic structures with professional interests has insulated urban school systems from reform. Reformers often have failed to initiate major change because they have tried to alter the behavior of professionals without doing very much about the structures in which they work, or they have concentrated on structural reforms with little attention to the interests of the professionals who work within the system.

By and large, reforms have failed to crack the skeletons of urban public school systems. Some historians argue that those skeletons had been erected by the latter-nineteenth century; others would date them a couple of decades later. The disagreement centers mainly on whether the differentiation of schooling in the early-twentieth century represents an extension of organizational principles, an elaboration of a preexisting model, or something novel. Although I take the former position, the disagreement does not weaken the general point: the structures of school systems are old, enduring, and resilient, and reform movements have failed to change their basic features. For the

[23] Lawrence A. Cremin, *The Transformation of the School: Progressivism in American Education, 1876–1957* (New York: Random House, 1965), pp. 348–49.
[24] Marvin Lazerson, *Origins of the Urban Public School: Public Education in Massachusetts, 1870–1915* (Cambridge: Harvard University Press, 1971).

most part, to change the metaphor, reforms have shifted around the furniture of education without moving walls or rebuilding the structures that contained it. The implementation of Chicago school reform is the first major assault on the walls and the first major reform to pay simultaneous attention to both the structure and profession of education. That is one reason why it is of such historic significance, and why the task it faces is so difficult.

Educational Reform as a Social Movement

Chicago school reform reflects and draws on the set of loosely interrelated urban social movements of the last three decades. In *City and the Grassroots*, Manuel Castells has described these urban social movements on a world scale.[25] In America, they include not only the Civil Rights Movement and the community action component of the War on Poverty but local "antigrowth" coalitions and neighborhood mobilizations around a variety of issues. Harry Boyte terms them, collectively, a "new citizens' movement."[26] Each movement has generated an indigenous leadership facilitating the coalescence of a new urban politics, which has scored local successes across the country.

Antigrowth protests have attacked the "growth coalitions" that sponsored urban redevelopment by replacing neighborhoods with office towers, expressways, and convention centers. At the same time, locally based, issue-specific, extraparty mobilizations of citizens have tried to stop an expressway, reclaim abandoned housing, end redlining by a bank, expand and reallocate services, improve the environment, extend citizen participation, and advance the cause of racial justice. (As Mike Davis shows, they also have appropriated the language of environmentalism and local democracy to preserve the economic and racial exclusiveness of their neighborhoods.)[27] Like most

---

[25] For an extended theoretical discussion of urban grass-roots social movements, see Manuel Castells, *The City and the Grassroots: A Cross-Cultural Theory of Urban Social Movements* (Berkeley and Los Angeles: University of California Press, 1983).

[26] Harry Boyte, *The Backyard Revolution: Understanding the New Citizen Movement* (Philadelphia: Temple University Press, 1980).

[27] Mike Davis, *City of Quartz: Excavating the Future in Los Angeles* (London: Verso, 1990).

social movements, these local mobilizations have served as agencies of adult education, for participation has demanded that members learn not only the tactics of social change but the substance of issues. By democratizing information, they have liberated citizens from dependence on official sources and incubated the leadership of the new urban politics.[28]

Despite the variety of their goals, these local movements transcend conventional party politics. They reveal a distrust of both large corporations and government bureaucracies and reflect a protest against remote organizations that swallow their dollars and structure their choices but deny them a voice. They express frustration, even rage, over the inability of ordinary citizens to influence the decisions that shape their lives. They call into question the authority of experts and the legitimacy of institutions.

Four features of social movements require special comment. Three are historical, one more recent. First, in America major social change has not originated with established political parties and institutions. The abolitionist movement, temperance, civil rights, the women's movement—all began outside conventional political channels and defied conventional political labels. Political parties adopted some of their demands when they became opportune; government became the vehicle for their translation into policy. But it did not incubate or nurture them.

Second, successful social movements have forged broad coalitions, often among unlikely partners. Coalitions, of course, have more leverage: they control more votes; they can mobilize diverse voices; and they legitimate what otherwise might be thought of as "special interests." David Rothman, for one, has documented the coalition of "conscience and convenience" that initiated reforms in the treatment of the mentally ill, criminals, and juvenile offenders during the Progressive Era; in the same years a coalition of employers, insurance companies, labor unions, academic experts, and reformers built the first step in America's welfare state: workmen's compensation. One could write the history of the Civil Rights Movement or the women's movement

---

[28] Castells, *City and the Grassroots*, discusses these processes.

from a similar perspective. Coalitions, however, remain fragile and often short-lived, and their splintering wounds the movements that they have sustained (a point to which I will return).[29]

Third is the difficulty of sustaining the zeal with which social movements begin. Usually movements follow a trajectory that Max Weber has described as the routinization of charisma; Ernst Troeltsch has called the transition from sect to church; and others have labeled the transformation as from cause into function. Whatever the label, the underlying dynamic is the same: the replacement of the white-hot energy with which mobilizations begin by organization and routine and the consequent translation of original purpose into institutional maintenance.[30]

Fourth, recent social movements have called on a new body of alternative experts. Whether they are protesting the environmental impact of an expressway, the dangers of a nuclear power plant, or the impact of urban renewal on affordable housing, activists require data. They need data both to argue for alternatives and to challenge the experts supporting the agencies and institutions they oppose. Alternative experts based in advocacy groups, new institutes, and universities now provide them with sophisticated support. At first, reliance on experts seems to contradict the demystification of professionalism and "objectivity" and the emphasis on grass-roots citizen participation and control that are at the core of urban social movements. The point, though, is more subtle. Recent social movements are helping to redefine the meaning and role of professionals and expert knowledge rather than to simply reproduce conventional relationships between knowledge and action. This redefinition, however, remains experimental, inchoate, still lacking clear formulations and models.[31] (For one model,

[29] David J. Rothman, *Conscience and Convenience: The Asylum and Its Alternatives in Progressive America* (Boston: Little, Brown, 1980); Roy Lubove, *The Struggle for Social Security, 1900–1935* (Cambridge: Harvard University Press, 1968).

[30] An example of this process in the field of social work is described in Roy Lubove, *The Professional Altruist: The Emergence of Social Work as a Career, 1880–1930* (Cambridge: Harvard University Press, 1965).

[31] On the relations between social science experts and public policy, a work I have found especially useful is Charles E. Lindblom and David K. Cohen, *Usable Knowledge: Social Science and Social Problem Solving* (New Haven: Yale University Press, 1965); in Chicago the major "alternative expert" advocacy organization supporting school re-

social movements might look to the "feminist" combination of research and advocacy in the early twentieth century, eloquently described by Robyn Muncy.)[32]

In every way, Chicago school reform fits the model of an urban social movement. It holds the bureaucratic, centralized structure of schooling partly accountable for educational failure; attacks the authority of school professionals and the school district's experts; redistributes power to parents and community representatives; and asserts the capacity of ordinary citizens to reach intelligent decisions about educational policy. A broad coalition outside conventional politics (business leaders together with parent and community groups and representatives of minority organizations) formulated a demand for radical school reform and seized a moment of widespread disgust following a teacher's strike to persuade the legislature to meet its demands. The coalition made its case with the help of alternative experts who provided authoritative data on educational failure and technical assistance in drafting new legislation. In the process, school reform has become a historic experiment in adult education, as its roughly six thousand Local School Council members have confronted, and often mastered, issues of management, finance, and educational policy.

. . . . .

On our first trip to Chicago, we took a taxi directly from the airport to the Dumas School, where, we had been told, we would find an exciting principal, Sylvia Peters, implementing reform. As our taxi pulled up to the school, adjacent to one of the city's largest public housing projects, friendly students rushed to take our luggage. In the school, a man dressed in formal clothes, like the doorman in an expensive condominium (we later learned he was the security guard), directed us to the principal's office. Sylvia Peters needed to attend to the opening of the school day before she could talk with us, but she introduced us to a member of the Local School Council, a

---

form is Designs for Change, Donald R. Moore, executive director. Hess discusses Designs' role in *School Restructuring* as do several of the individuals interviewed for O'Connell, *School Reform*.

[32] Robyn Muncy, *Creating a Female Dominion in American Reform, 1860–1935* (New York: Oxford University Press, 1991).

grandmother, probably in her sixties, raising the child of a daughter who had died. A short, shy woman with wispy gray hair, she said she was glad to meet some educators because she wanted opinions on the merits of the whole language approach to teaching reading, which the LSC was debating. Later in the morning we met the chair of the LSC, an impressive woman in her thirties who told us how her position had required her to learn to run a meeting, read a school budget, and think about educational issues. In the next two years, we heard many similar stories.

. . . . .

Special circumstances in Chicago facilitated the success of the school reform movement: both the election and, as I noted earlier, ironically, the subsequent death of Harold Washington, a committed, charismatic mayor, himself outside the main political machine, who first assembled an education summit; a rich legacy of community organizing facilitated especially by the late Saul Alinsky; and an enlightened, active philanthropic community led by foundations organized into the Donors Forum. In its first year, the base of support for school reform broadened to include at least rhetorical commitment from virtually every major constituency in the city. To its supporters, school reform became a cause that they sustained with energy, dedication, and long, unpaid hours of work. In the process, they built a social movement across the lines of race and class that usually divide the populations of this and other cities.[33]

Race and Ethnicity: Schools as "Contested Terrain"

The politics of Chicago school reform as both process and movement remain partly a politics of race. There, as in other cities, ethnic and racial groups always have viewed schools as "contested terrain" in their competition for resources, rewards, and recognition. Alone

[33] Paul Kleppner, *Chicago Divided: The Making of a Black Mayor* (De Kalb: Northern Illinois University Press, 1985); Robert A. Slayton, *Back of the Yards: The Making of a Local Democracy* (Chicago: University of Chicago Press, 1986); Gregory D. Squires, Larry Bennett, Kathleen McCourt, and Philip Nyden, *Chicago: Race, Class, and the Response to Urban Decline* (Philadelphia: Temple University Press, 1987), pp. 127–51; Hess, *School Restructuring*, pp. 120–21, 168.

among major institutions, schools, as Ira Katznelson explains, unite the otherwise bifurcated politics of neighborhood and workplace that have characterized America's "city trenches" since the mid-nineteenth century. For Katznelson, the politics of neighborhood, channeled through political machines, has focused on issues of ethnicity, race, and territoriality; the politics of work, expressed through trade unions, has concerned jobs, income, and other matters related to class. The split between them has prevented the formation of a political movement based on class, or a labor party, as has formed in other Western industrial democracies. Only schools transcend the bifurcated politics of America's cities because they link concerns of home and neighborhood with those of class. For this reason, they stand as outposts fought over in the ongoing wars for survival and dominance among competing ethnic and racial groups in America's cities.[34]

In Chicago as elsewhere, recent demographic history and the redefinition of urban space have heightened struggles over the contested terrain of schooling. Population movement constitutes the first force: the great post–World War II migration of African Americans into Chicago, the more recent arrival of Latinos, and the exodus of whites. By shifting the political as well as the demographic balance in the city, these migratory patterns have changed the rules of the contest, the major issues at stake, and the identities of the players. Within the city, a new social ecology has emerged: vast areas of concentrated poverty and transitional zones where African Americans and either whites or Latinos struggle for dominance. In these transitional areas the racial struggles around schooling assume their most intense and visible form.[35]

But racial struggles permeate almost all educational politics, often in ironic ways. Desegregation, of course, fueled modern racial politics. In the South, desegregating schools sometimes precipitated the loss of

[34] The phrase "contested terrain" is from Richard C. Edwards, *Contested Terrain: The Transformation of the Workplace in the Twentieth Century* (New York: Basic Books, 1979); Ira Katznelson, *City Trenches: Urban Politics and the Patterning of Class in the United States* (New York: Pantheon, 1981); Ira Katznelson and Margaret Weir, *Schooling for All: Class, Race, and the Decline of the Democratic Ideal* (New York: Basic Books, 1985).

[35] Squires et al., *Chicago*, pp. 23–126; Nicholas Lemann, *The Promised Land: The Great Black Migration and How It Changed America* (New York: Alfred A. Knopf, 1991).

jobs for black educators, a theme, albeit played out differently, in Chicago school reform as well. In Chicago, the school district resisted desegregation for years, defying the law with one tactic or another. At the same time, the city government resisted building public housing until it could assure its racial segregation. These fierce, bitter battles around racial issues culminated in the 1983 election of Harold Washington, the city's first African American mayor, who inherited a city where each year white flight (the public school system now has about 15 percent white students) left the issue of racial integration increasingly moot. The city's new demography combined with affirmative action to put African Americans in the school district's administration. In fact, in the 1970s and 1980s, the school system facilitated upward mobility among the city's African Americans. It was their misfortune, however, to inherit an educationally bankrupt school district at the moment of school reform. When reformers attacked the school bureaucracy, they assaulted African Americans; when in its first year school reform eliminated about five hundred central office jobs, most of those cut were black. For this reason, at first organizations representing middle-class African Americans remained distant from, if not hostile to, school reform. They argued that reformers had excluded them from negotiations with the state legislature. Some contended it was no coincidence that reformers launched an attack on the central administration only when its color had changed to black.[36]

The first contemporary racial struggles over the contested terrain of schooling focused on access: eliminating both legal and de facto segregation and questioning testing and tracking practices that seemed to discriminate against minority children. In the 1960s, power also emerged as a major issue, expressed in attacks on educational bureaucracy, calls for parent and community control, and experiments in decentralization. With the retreat from the spirit of the Great Society and the misuse of the example of New York City to discredit it, community control, unlike desegregation, almost vanished as an issue. Only

---

[36] Paul E. Peterson, *School Politics, Chicago Style* (Chicago: University of Chicago Press, 1976); Arnold R. Hirsch, *Making the Second Ghetto: Race and Housing in Chicago, 1940–1960* (New York: Cambridge University Press, 1983); Kleppner, *Chicago Divided*, pp. 32–63.

recently has it reappeared with the surging interest in school-based management and educational restructuring, of which Chicago forms the most dramatic example.

Early in the century, debates about African American education also included topics of curriculum and purpose. The disagreement over industrial education between Booker T. Washington and W. E. B. Dubois defined the two ends of a spectrum dividing African American educators throughout the country. With the dissipation of the issue, the struggles around segregation and control overwhelmed the question of content. Recently, however, calls for "diversity" and an African-centered curriculum have refocused debate on the content of schooling. The reasons are various: the virtual disappearance of desegregation as an issue, the decline of white control over schooling, a search for ways to build pride and self-esteem in African American children, a belief that conventional curricula rest on a constricted, inaccurate view of history and culture, and, of course, the rise of a national movement championing multiculturalism and diversity.[37]

The debate over an African-centered curriculum adds to the issues fueling the racial politics of school reform in Chicago. Although a racial politics did not emerge with school reform, in the last few years racial politics has assumed a new shape. The terrain remains contested, but the landmarks, rules, and even the identity of the contestants are not so clear. In its racial politics, the process of Chicago school reform also stands on the edge of history.[38]

The Revitalization of the Public Sphere

As both a legislative achievement and a process of educational improvement, Chicago school reform stands as the major alternative to the assimilation of schooling to a market model. If it fails, the advocates of "choice" across public and private schools will inherit the

[37] In Chicago, the movement for an African-centered curriculum is led by the Center for Inner City Studies of Northeastern University.

[38] The standard analysis of educational politics in Chicago in the pre–school reform era is Peterson, *School Politics*; for historical background on the politics of educational reform, see Paul E. Peterson, *The Politics of School Reform, 1870–1940* (Chicago: University of Chicago Press, 1985).

field. The momentum of recent history works against Chicago school reform because of the degradation of the public sphere (discussed in chapter 2) that taints public education along with government and other aspects of civic life.

Public has shifted its meaning throughout American history, and relations between public and private have remained protean, their boundaries always contested and renegotiated. (Chapter 1 tells some of this story as it is reflected in the history of welfare.) In early modern England and colonial America, *public* referred to education carried on in a school instead of at home with a tutor. In the early-nineteenth century, it signified schools open to a broad section of the population and either free or inexpensive. New York State at first tried to provide secondary education by giving state funds to privately owned and managed academies. In New York City the New York Public School Society was a voluntary association that provided schooling for the city's children with money from the state. In these early years, *public* often was equated with *pauper*, because only the poorest children in cities received free education.[39]

To create common schools that embraced all classes, the first genera- tion of school reformers worked to break the equation of *public* with *pauper*. Their remarkable success resulted not only in a new public institution but in a new definition of *public* as combining both the fi- nancing and control of schools. Institutions founded, controlled, and administered by voluntary associations no longer could claim public status, even when they received most or all their funding from govern- ment sources. This definition of *public* has persisted. It has succeeded so completely that we accept it as natural, as the only meaning conso- nant with American political culture, when it is, instead, a product created to suit a set of historical circumstances.

The new antebellum definition of *public* reflected optimism about the possibilities of democracy, pride in government, and a robust civic culture. In the same years, as state and local governments assumed new social responsibilities, they built new institutions for the sick,

---

[39] I have discussed this at greater length in *Reconstructing American Education*; on the New York Public School Society, see Kaestle, *The Evolution of an Urban School System*.

mentally ill, poor, delinquent, and criminal. The monumental architecture of these institutions (even, often, poorhouses, discussed in chapter 1) attested to the civic pride and optimism about the capacity of government they embodied. The high proportion of eligible voters who cast their ballots in local elections signified an active political culture and a belief that government mattered. The parades and processions that marked every holiday and notable event testified to a collective civic life acted "in public."[40]

By the early-twentieth century, observers wrote about city government as the conspicuous failure of American democracy. Electoral participation had declined. City governments preoccupied with order had channeled popular festivities into bland, controlled rituals. Reformers viewed major institutions—penitentiaries, mental hospitals, reformatories, poorhouses—as warehouses incapable of effecting rehabilitation. Welfare reformers feared the incompetence and corruption of government would undermine any form of public relief. Only public schools and hospitals retained their hold on public esteem. Advances in medical science and the reorganization of medical practice improved the public standing of hospitals.[41] Despite a barrage of criticism, public schools could claim unique advantages: they drew in children across class boundaries; they appeared to deliver the credentials increasingly necessary for economic mobility; and they offered a relatively cheap and nonredistributive way to ameliorate crime and poverty and to acculturate immigrants to America.

As the functions of state and local government expanded throughout the first several decades of the twentieth century, public schools managed to stave off further erosion of their legitimacy and support. American cities retained a public sphere that—if it excited few and annoyed many—at least appeared capable of reform. Civic groups

[40] On the architecture of nineteenth-century municipal institutions, see Eric Monkkonen, "Nineteenth-Century Institutions Dealing with the Urban Underclass," in Katz, *"Underclass" Debate*; on parades and processions, see Susan G. Davis, *Parades and Power: Street Theater in Nineteenth-Century Philadelphia* (Philadelphia: Temple University Press, 1986).

[41] Charles Rosenberg, *The Care of Strangers: The Rise of America's Hospital System* (New York: Basic Books, 1987).

132

that wanted to improve cities tried to reform public practices and institutions, not to replace them with private alternatives.

Exactly when support for the public sphere began to erode is unclear, although the 1960s probably marks the turning point. But its effects, as I observed in chapter 1, are unmistakable. One institution after another has lost its hold on public confidence. To many people, civic government appears hopeless. As a result, reformers increasingly seek answers to civic problems in a market model that contracts the functions of government to the private sector.[42] In education, the Civil Rights Movement helped expose the contradictions between the democratic promise of public schooling and its segregated, tracked, unequal reality. Middle-class migration to suburbs robbed public schools of strong supporters and weakened their tax base. Court decisions prevented state legislatures from forcing suburbs to share their resources with cities. Increased poverty confronted city schools with heightened problems. Bureaucratic structures hampered school systems' response to their new context. In the early-twentieth century, one young woman had no difficulty controlling classes of fifty or seventy students in city schools, which were remarkable for their order. By the 1970s, students and teachers feared violence in classrooms and hallways, and armed guards patrolled their corridors. Critics complained that urban schools at best functioned as custodial warehouses, keeping youngsters off the streets but teaching them very little. In many cities, almost all parents who could afford the expense sent their children to private or parochial schools. As a result, in education, *public* returned to its early-nineteenth-century equation with *pauper*.

Along with other urban institutions, public schools had lost the legitimacy that had sustained their hold on public esteem and the public purse. Urban Americans now lived with a degraded public sphere that they increasingly rejected. Many, reading recent history as showing public schools impervious to reform, looked longingly, and with rose-tinted glasses, at private and parochial schools, and they defined re-

[42] Jeffrey R. Henig, *Rethinking School Choice: Limits of the Market Metaphor* (Princeton: Princeton University Press, 1993).

form as giving parents tax dollars to send their children to whatever schools they chose.

School reformers in Chicago share the prevailing criticisms of public schools and the conclusion that earlier reforms by and large failed. They, too, see the school bureaucracy as impervious to change, and they advocate radical restructuring. The difference is, they reject public-private choice as the direction. Their commitment to the interconnections among community, democracy, and education leads them away from market models. They believe public-private choice will increase inequalities; they fear that any model of choice, introduced prematurely, will undermine the efforts of local communities to improve their schools. They seek the revitalization of the public sphere, not its abandonment.[43]

The Limits of Educational Reform: Are Schools the Solution to Social Problems?

As a process, Chicago school reform unfolds within an arena defined by three shifting boundaries: demography and space comprise two of them. The third is the city's restructured economy. Like other major cities, Chicago has lost much of its manufacturing base. In its emergent form, Chicago is a postindustrial city with an economy rooted in finance, real estate, education, health care, and other services. The shift has profound implications for education.

It helps explain, for instance, the involvement of the business community in school reform. Part of its interest derives from familiar concerns about the availability of a skilled workforce now and in the next century. But the business community's sympathy for school reform also reflects the reorganization of contemporary corporations. Sooner than educators, business leaders realized the drawbacks of excessive centralization and bureaucracy. Many have drawn on a new organizational literature that emphasizes flexibility and participation to reform

[43] "Thinking about the *V*-Word" (unsigned editorial), *Chicago Tribune*, May 17, 1991, p. 26; Diana Nelson, "School Reform as Superior to Vouchers," *Chicago Tribune*, June 3, 1991, p. 14; G. Alfred Hess Jr., "Too Much Democracy or Too Little?" (address to the Legal Forum at the University of Chicago Law School, October 27, 1990).

their firms. For them, school reformers' assault on bureaucracy and centralization resonates with their experience conducting business in a postindustrial world.[44]

Business leaders probably always have had their own organizational models in mind when they thought about schooling, and throughout American history they have participated actively in educational reform. Indeed, attempts to recast schooling have occurred during each major economic restructuring in American history. Urban school systems emerged first in the mid-nineteenth century during the transition to industrial capitalism. In the late-nineteenth and early-twentieth centuries, the great wave of Progressive-Era reform accompanied the growth of giant national corporations and changes in manufacturing organization and technology. In each instance, advocates argued for educational reforms necessitated, they said, by unprecedented developments and opportunities.

Advocates of educational reform, however, pressed for more than an appropriate fit between schooling and new forms of economic organization. They also asserted the unique capacity of schools to solve the great social problems occasioned by the recurrent transformations of America: crime, poverty, unassimilated immigrants, weakened families, unreliable workers. In the process, they oversold the potential of schooling. One result has been recurrent rounds of attack by critics and rebuttals by educators faced with the repeated need to justify failure.[45]

Like its predecessors, Chicago school reform, as a process of change, promises a great deal. But it exists in the context of deindustrialization, segregation, racism, and concentrated poverty now compounded by fiscal crisis. It confronts urban schools that have resisted fundamental change for decades. With even the most enlightened leadership and all the best breaks, schools by themselves cannot dent the poverty, crime, and racial isolation that disfigure major American cities. In fact, unrealistic expectations for schools can retard the amelioration of social problems, as has happened throughout America's past,

[44] Hess, *School Restructuring*, pp. 117–18.
[45] Henry J. Perkinson, *The Imperfect Panacea: American Faith in Education, 1865–1965* (New York: Random House, 1968).

by obscuring the difficult redistributive issues that underlie them. What American school reform has lacked throughout its history, and Chicago has yet to offer, is a set of appropriate and realistic expectations, an ambitious but prudent sense of the outer limits of educational change.

Implications of History

No policy recommendations flow automatically from this attempt to situate Chicago school reform as legislation, process, and movement within American social history. However, a set of questions and cautions flow from this attempt to view Chicago school reform as history.

First, the origins of bureaucracy and the emergence of expertise: urban school bureaucracies have absorbed most previous reforms, undercutting their original purposes and transforming them to fit existing structures. How can Chicago school reformers avoid this mimetic pattern of reform? Past school reform has failed, too, because it has placed excessive and unrealistic demands on teachers. Can Chicago school reform as process discover a responsible and equitable way to energize, and often reeducate, teachers? Professionalism and expertise frequently have served as ideologies to advance the career interests of school personnel and distance them from the parents and communities they have served. Still, few would deny the importance of experience, the relevance of advanced knowledge and skills, and the importance of some research. How can school reform negotiate a balance between the appropriate exercise of expertise and democratic control?

Second, education as a social movement: the coalitions that sponsor major reforms reflect divergent interests, and for that reason they almost always have remained fragile, splintering eventually along their fault lines, with major influence resting with the most powerful partners. What can hold together the cross-class, multiracial constituency that sponsored the legislation creating Chicago school reform, and what will be the consequences if it splinters? Social movements that start in a blaze of passion almost always lose their zeal. As they become routine, they dissipate not only their energy but their purpose. Can Chicago school reform as a movement defy the conventional sociology of social movements by finding ways to retain its energy and passion? As a social movement, Chicago school reform has drawn on a set of alternative experts whose assistance has proved essential but whose ongoing role remains unclear. Can it define a role for its alternative experts that links knowledge to social action without sacrificing the distinctive contributions of either? (The short history of the Consortium on Chicago School Research gives grounds for optimism that the city's research and reform communities will devise a unique, supportive relationship.)

Third, schools as contested terrain: American urban schools always have served as contested terrain in racial and ethnic politics. Schools constitute one forum in which participants in a diverse polity confront their differences and negotiate their aspirations. But racial contests also have ripped communities and schools apart. Can Chicago school reformers find constructive ways to mediate the tensions among the city's racial and ethnic groups and help them realize their goals? (Here grounds for optimism exist. By mid-1994, racial tensions around reform had moderated significantly.) The implementation of Chicago school reform blocked one road to African American mobility by cutting jobs in the central administration. Whatever its gains for children and parents, it represents a setback for one segment of the city's African American middle class. Can school reformers find a way to balance demands for equity and mobility with a redistribution of power to local schools and the communities they serve?

Fourth, the revitalization of the public sphere: Chicago school reform represents the major alternative to private-public choice as a plan for restructuring urban schools. It inherits the legacy of failed educational reforms. It confronts the momentum of privatization. It is surrounded by failed urban institutions and a degraded public sphere. Can its advocates make a convincing intellectual case for rebuilding the public sphere? Can they stave off the forces of choice long enough to improve their local schools? Can they create a sphere for democracy that resists the market?[46]

---

[46] The intellectual basis for restricting the market to its appropriate sphere is articulated with force and clarity by Michael Walzer in *Spheres of Justice: A Defense of Pluralism and Equality* (New York: Basic Books, 1983); see also the criticism of market-based models in Henig, *Rethinking School Choice*.

Fifth, the limits of educational reform: The rhetoric of Chicago school reform sometimes slips into the language of unrealistic expectations that in earlier periods has undercut educational reform and retarded effective solutions to social problems. Can Chicago school reformers develop appropriate and realistic expectations for the city's schools? Although school reform by itself cannot solve Chicago's great problems, no big city in American history has mobilized a comparable social movement around educational reform. With its roots reaching deep into the interstices of the city's ethnic and racial communities, can school reform become a catalyst for an even more ambitious social movement that directly addresses the city's poverty, joblessness, and continued legacy of racism?[47]

These are some of the challenges that emerge from appreciating Chicago's daring, exciting, and unprecedented adventure in school reform as history. How well have the challenges been met?[48] What are measures of success or failure? Clearly, developing appropriate assessments remains an urgent problem. Assessments should conceive of school reform as a process, not a series of events with a definable beginning and end. If it works, school reform never will be over. Instead, it will release local energies in a continuous process of school improvement that will not be "finished." We have been told that about one hundred schools, or roughly one-fifth of the system, have seized the opportunity offered by reform to begin significant educational change in processes of learning and teaching.

In a July 1993 report on the city's elementary schools, Anthony Bryk and his colleagues in the Chicago Consortium on School Research ask, "Is the restructuring of the Chicago public school system evolving in ways that can lead to major improvements in student learning? We answer yes." They estimate conservatively that one-third of the elementary schools most in need of change, "where student assessment reports are significantly below national norms ... have developed strong democratic participation within their school community that is now focused on a systematic approach to whole school improve-

[47] For an assessment of Chicago school reform after its first two years, see G. Alfred Hess Jr., "School Restructuring, Chicago Style: A Midway Report" (paper presented at the American Anthropological Association meeting, November 22, 1991).

[48] The assessment that follows is an adaptation of Michael B. Katz, Elaine Simon, and Michelle Fine, "Memo to Chicago," *Catalyst* 4:9 (June 1993): 14–17.

ment." Another third share some of these features but have not moved as far along in the process of improvement. The improvements in these schools validate the theory underlying reform because where "enhanced participation has emerged . . . fundamental organizational changes are highly likely, and 'best' instruction practices are now being introduced."[49] Given the short history of Chicago school reform—two years, at most, since schools were sufficiently reorganized to begin educational change—and the historic resistance of urban school systems, the accomplishments reported by the Consortium appear hopeful to a cautious observer, extraordinary to an optimist.

One can also measure success by what has not happened. Professional educators, in the aggregate, worried about having to respond to idiosyncratic, unreasonable, educationally unsound demands from "uninformed" parents and community members. In fact, not only have parents and community members proved responsible; they have been educationally conservative. The problem has not been an excess but a deficit of imagination.

Others worried that four-year contracts decided by local school councils and the lack of tenure would render the job of principal unattractive. In fact, dozens of candidates willing to play by the rules of school reform have applied for every principal opening. Indeed, surveys show that principals, elementary school teachers (high school teachers have not yet been surveyed), and local school council members approve of reform.

Everyone we have listened to talks about how to "make reform work." No one suggests reversing it, such as by recentralizing the system or taking power away from parents. What has been accomplished and taken for granted in Chicago scarcely can be imagined in other American cities. That Chicago implemented the administrative and structural aspects of reform so quickly and completely is itself an amazing and historic achievement. In Chicago, debates about public education assume the existence of reform. This is one measure of its success.

Yet another indicator of success concerns community discourse

[49] Anthony Bryk et al., *A View from the Elementary Schools: The State of Reform in Chicago* (report of the Steering Committee Consortium on Chicago School Research, July 1993), p. 37.

about public education in Chicago. School reform there has stimulated constructive open conversations about education. In what other major city would a public television station devote nearly six hours of Saturday programming to three panel discussions on public education? In what other city could this forum attract the governor, the mayor, a foundation president, the leader of a major national union, corporate chief executives, nationally known school reformers, and many others?

Why has not even more happened at local schools? Why has not change been faster? Part of the reason reflects the challenge to the imagination posed by the opportunity for school reform. Prisoners of a model of education over a century old, most of us find it nearly impossible even to imagine alternative ways of learning and teaching; socialized in one powerful and pervasive system, we fear the risks in trying something wholly novel. One great problem of Chicago school reform is finding ways to foster alternative visions of education and, at the same time, to allay the anxieties that radical change evokes.

By their training and work experience, not to mention their own education, teachers have difficulty envisioning radical alternatives because the culture of their schools discourages conversations, professional development, and risk taking. Many individual teachers are remarkable; most school cultures are stifling. Local School Councils, which have remained relatively isolated from one another, also find difficulty envisioning radical educational change. Truly, the loneliness and isolation that are key components of the culture of public education discourage innovation and risk.

By failing to stimulate new visions and to nurture and protect risk takers, the central administration missed an opportunity to foster reform. Its potential role as a catalyst for radical educational visions became unimaginable, for either its supporters or opponents, in most debates about the role of the central administration. Therefore, it falls to principals to take the lead in fostering educational vision and staff development. Indeed, we have been struck by the centrality of principals to school success or failure. Chicago school reform redefines every aspect of a principal's job. It increases principals' risks and opportunities; it provides them with new masters and greater autonomy;

it demands extraordinary amounts of time and energy. Some principals have seized these new challenges; others have not. Appointing a principal remains the most important job of a local school council.

The preoccupation with conventional measures of assessment also discourages innovation and risk. Faced with evaluation by national or statewide standardized test scores, the safest course for teachers and principals often seems the most familiar one. Still, the need to assess achievement and performance cannot be evaded. Although many educators and reformers in Chicago and elsewhere accurately criticize conventional measures, no alternative has been systematically adopted. Some educators are experimenting with promising alternatives more suited to current thinking about teaching and learning, such as portfolio-based assessment, but these are not yet used widely. If gauging improvement by standardized test scores appears an inadequate measure of the progress of Chicago school reform, the development of alternatives demands urgent attention. Reform came into being because of poor student outcomes. The question of achievement must be addressed vigorously and creatively.

From whatever perspective one takes and by whatever measures one uses, some schools are performing badly. It could be that they need more time or new principals. But, eventually, the question of what to do about nonperforming schools will require an answer. The issue is crucial in part because of the need to find some way to pressure recalcitrant schools to improve and in part because Chicago must show it has a democratic means for holding its schools accountable. Only when they are convinced that the system has a commitment to accountability will many in the state legislature be willing to provide more money for Chicago's schools. The question of how to improve nonperforming schools plagues the nation, as well. Local control does not automatically solve the problem. Typically, parents in a neighborhood are loath to close down their local school. Leadership, therefore, must come from some other sources. As virtually everyone concerned with education in the city has recognized, Chicago needs to create mechanisms whereby poorly performing schools are supported, transformed, or closed and reopened.

Of all the issues threatening Chicago school reform, the most serious is its budget crisis. If the resolution of the crisis results in the erosion of reform—and this is one scenario we have heard from more than one well-informed observer—the tendency will be to blame the conceptual underpinnings of reform and to discredit the capacity of parents and the potential of local democracy. Such a reading would be wrong. The budget crisis has structural origins that have nothing to do with reform.

In fact, with support, Chicago school reform will legitimate local democracy. As it trains local school council members in parliamentary procedures, the analysis of budgets, the selection of principals, the evaluation of curricula and many others matters, Chicago school reform is a vast engine of adult education for developing effective citizens. The pressing question for American government, Robert Bellah and his associates have written, "is not just what government should do but how it can do it in a way that strengthens the initiative and participation of citizens, both as individuals and within their communities and associations, rather than reducing them to the status of clients."[50] This is one question that Chicago school reform promises to anwer. If it revitalizes public education, Chicago school reform will become a model for how to reverse the slide into privatization and restore the preconditions of an effective public sphere in America. This is why it must succeed.

. . . . .

On our trips to Chicago, the most interesting experiences usually have happened unplanned. One night, finding ourselves without an appointment, we persuaded one of the Chicago Panel's researchers to take us to a Local School Council meeting at a school he was following. In the gym/ auditorium of the school, adjacent to a large public housing project, we found the parents, all African American or Latino, and teachers gathered to interview candidates for principal (and eat excellent refreshments baked by the parents). The Local School Council had decided not to renew the contract of the current principal, and he had left precipitously in the midst of the school year. The school was not doing well. Parents knew it; so did

[50] Robert Bellah et al., *The Good Society* (New York: Random House, 1991), p. 27.

teachers. Morale was very low. A search committee of the LSC had selected four finalists for the principal's job and invited them to make presentations to the larger school community. All four—three African American men and one woman—sat on the stage waiting their turn to speak for five minutes. They had been asked to talk about why they wanted to be principal, what their ideas and their qualifications were. After they had spoken, the audience asked probing questions. Each of the candidates impressed us as capable, articulate, and intelligent. The woman candidate, however, seemed to us to stand out from the others. Exhilarated by the exercise in democracy we had witnessed, we wondered which candidate the LSC would choose. We learned soon after that it was the woman. Eager to know what impact she would have on the school, we began to visit it a couple of times a year. On each visit we observed progress, much better teacher morale, new educational programs, improved safety in the corridors and classrooms. At this writing, the school, as the principal and teachers know, still has a long way to go, but the energetic, creative new principal has initiated a promising process of educational change. In less than two years, the school has become a different place. In stories like these, we find hope for the success of Chicago school reform.

Surviving Poverty

THE SUMMER OF 1962 changed my life. I had spent the 1961–62 academic year in the Master of Arts in Teaching Program at Harvard's Graduate School of Education and was slated to spend the next year in England on a fellowship, a wonderful opportunity as well as an interlude in which to think about the next steps in a career. The year in the School of Education had disrupted my plans to become a "straight" historian and opened a wealth of possibilities that spanned the spectrum from administration (elementary school principal? school superintendent?) to research (historian of education? reading specialist? educational anthropologist?). Nearing the completion of my internship teaching history in Winchester High School, I had to find a summer job to sustain my family in the months before we left for England. On the bulletin board in the School of Education was a notice that the Cambridge Neighborhood House was looking for a playschool director.

For some reason, possibly because I always liked working with little children, the job intrigued me. Located in a dismal area of the city, not far from MIT, the 'Hood, as it was known locally, stood across from two big housing projects, one built in the 1930s, early in the history of public housing, the other a couple of decades later. The 'Hood, which claimed to be the oldest settlement house in the United States, occupied the only large house remaining in the neighborhood. Aside from a secretary, its full-time permanent staff, as I recall, consisted of its director, Elsa Baldwin, who, in turn, was looked after by an enormous, forbidding mutt named Max. It was rumored that Elsa had an apartment somewhere; I always found her at the 'Hood. She was, I thought, the last link between the founders of the settlement movement and the present, as close as I ever would come to Jane Addams.

The neighborhood was not especially safe, although by the standards of today's inner cities it appears, in retrospect, comparatively tame. Most of the residents were white, with only a few African Americans scattered throughout the projects. The main trouble came from the knots of teenage men (*gang* is too formal a term) hanging around, unemployed, bored, and sullen. As I parked my car in front of the 'Hood for the first time, they watched with a mixture of suspicion and curiosity as I pounded on the impenetrable metal door that always was locked after hours. In the course of the evening, as my interview with Elsa progressed, they would take my car for a joyride and bang it up. My relatively calm reaction, I think, more than my degrees or ideas, won me an instant job offer.

Elsa wanted to start a summer program that combined daytime activities for local children with evening activities for and home visiting with their parents. The program would be virtually free of charge. (This was before Operation Headstart, which her ideas anticipated; I still have no idea how she financed it.) She expected the director, whom she clearly preferred not to have formal training in social work, to plan the program, hire and train the staff, recruit the children, teach, work with parents, and spend most weekdays and evenings at the 'Hood. For this she offered sixty dollars a week.

I wanted the job very much, but it seemed an indulgence. I had a family and needed money. Even as an undergraduate working part-time selling encyclopedias, I had averaged a good deal more than sixty dollars each week. Conflicted, I went for advice to my former senior tutor at Harvard, William R. Taylor. He told me to take the job. I'd spent a lot of time, he said, doing things I didn't like; I was entitled to this one.

The summer was magical. Somehow I recruited a dedicated, talented, energetic staff. We drummed up enough children to fill an old yellow school bus, which defined our capacity. We alternated activities in the 'Hood, on its hot asphalt playground, with trips to playgrounds, amusement parks, places to swim or walk in the woods. We brought in physicians to examine the children, visited their parents, listened to their problems, and invited them to programs at the 'Hood. The children and their parents, mostly warm, open, and generous, became our friends.

We could do little, if anything, about their real problems, we all

145

soon realized. This was the frustration of the job. They struggled to survive on inadequate welfare payments, lived in badly maintained public housing, sent their children to ineffective schools, lacked opportunities or training for jobs, could not afford medical or dental care, and were buffeted by social service, educational, and law enforcement bureaucracies over which they had no influence. This was a course not taught at Harvard: what it took to survive poverty. Whatever I did as a career, I knew, should be in some way relevant to the experience of my new friends at the 'Hood.

The other great lesson of the summer concerned stereotypes. I had begun with fairly conventional "liberal" ideas, which, at the time, pivoted around the culture of poverty, or "cultural deprivation." My initial assumptions patronized the people of the neighborhood; I did not think them really competent; I had no sense of them as individuals; they were, in my imagination, victims. The experience of working with them shook all these assumptions. The children, by and large, were wonderful, as bright, eager, and trusting as any others. Their parents cared deeply about them. Their daily struggle to survive took intelligence, cleverness, and energy. Yes, they seemed at times overwhelmed; forces they could not entirely comprehend circumscribed their well-being and opportunities. Still, living in circumstances that would have sapped my energy and soured my personality, most of them proved resilient and resourceful, gritty, smart survivors of urban poverty. Knowing them left me an unreconstructed democrat, convinced of the capacity within ordinary people, ready to challenge the image of the passive, incompetent poor so pervasive in journalism, other mass media, and social science.

An important tradition in social science challenges these stereotypes of poor people as passive and incompetent. (The older images, however, persist in some social science, as in the work of the influential political scientist Lawrence Mead, who describes the nonworking poor as "incompetent.")[1] The work of ethnographers and, more recently, social historians describes survival strategies, reveals intricate social structures and networks within the poorest communities, and

---

[1] Lawrence Mead, *The New Politics of Poverty: The Nonworking Poor in America* (New York: Basic Books, 1992).

uncovers a distinctive politics among the poor. For example, Eliot Liebow and Elijah Anderson reconstructed, respectively, the social order among street-corner men and within a South Chicago bar. Carol Stack discovered networks of mutual assistance among poor women living on welfare. Kathryn Neckerman and Mark Stern have analyzed the survival strategies of poor families early in the twentieth century; Christine Stansell has traced them among women in mid-nineteenth-century New York City; Jacqueline Jones has written their history in African American families from slavery through the twentieth century; Robin D. G. Kelley has applied anthropologist James Scott's notion of "infrapolitics" to describe a distinctive political tradition among poor African Americans in the twentieth century. Frances Fox Piven and Richard Cloward have written a history of "poor people's movements"; Carl Nightingale has recovered the experience of African American youth in Philadelphia from 1940 to 1990.[2]

Part of the contribution of this literature rests in its restoration of agency and dignity to poor people. It has helped, as well, resolve a puzzle: How did families survive when, by all accounts, their incomes were below the amounts necessary for the minimum standard of living? It also is research with the potential, as yet largely untapped, to illuminate a very large practical and theoretical issue: How do social institutions interact with one another to shape the lives of individuals and families? Most historical or contemporary research on social institutions not only starts from the top down, that is, with a focus on official policy, reformers, administrators, and formal structure; it

[2] Elliot Liebow, *Tally's Corner: A Study of Negro Streetcorner Men* (Boston: Little, Brown, 1967); Elijah Anderson, *A Place on the Corner* (Chicago: University of Chicago Press, 1978); Carol B. Stack, *All Our Kin: Strategies for Survival in a Black Community* (New York: Harper and Row, 1974); Kathryn M. Neckerman, "The Emergence of 'Underclass' Family Patterns, 1900–1940," in Michael B. Katz, ed., *The "Underclass" Debate: Views from History* (Princeton: Princeton University Press, 1993), pp. 194–219; Mark J. Stern, "Poverty and Family Composition since 1940," in Katz, *"Underclass" Debate*, pp. 220–53; Christine Stansell, *City of Women: Sex and Class in New York, 1789–1860* (New York: Knopf, 1986); Jacqueline Jones, *Labor of Love, Labor of Sorrow: Black Women, Work and the Family from Slavery to the Present* (New York: Basic Books, 1985); Robin D. G. Kelley, "The Black Poor and the Politics of Opposition in a New South City," in Katz, *"Underclass" Debate*, pp. 293–333; Frances Fox Piven and Richard A. Cloward, *Poor People's Movements: Why They Succeed, How They Fail* (New York: Pantheon, 1977); Carl Husemoller Nightingale, *On the Edge: A History of Poor Black Children and Their American Dreams* (New York: Basic Books, 1993).

also concentrates on one institution at a time: welfare, the police, schools, hospitals. This is not, however, the way in which poor people experience the world. It matters little what institutional sponsors write about their goals, whether these agencies are "public" or "private," or how their internal administrative hierarchies are structured. What counts is what they do: what kind of help they offer; how accessible their services are; what conditions they attach to assistance. Institutions are landmarks on a terrain through which poor people must navigate in order to survive. Looked at this way, the important research questions are different from those that dominate conventional social science.

My own contribution to this redirection of perspective is an ongoing attempt to reconstruct the experience of people living in extreme poverty in New York City in the late-nineteenth and early-twentieth centuries. The stories that follow show some of what I have learned so far. Because they are stories that resonate with the issues addressed in the preceding chapters, they form a fitting ending for this book.[3]

SURVIVING POVERTY: THREE NEW YORK STORIES

Viewed from the vantage of a poor widow, an out-of-work express-man, or a fourteen-year-old worried about how his mother will pay the rent, early-twentieth-centry social institutions and policies for the poor appeared different than they did from the offices of New York's leading philanthropies, the city's Bureau of Dependent Children, a

---

[3] The stories narrated here are based on the case records of the Charity Organization Society of New York. The surviving COS case records are in the Rare Book and Manuscript Room of Butler Library, Columbia University. In some instances, I have supplemented the case records with material from manuscript censuses, assessment rolls, insurance maps, and mortgage records as well as from institutional sources. The best single overview of the charity organization movement is Frank Dekker Watson, *The Charity Organization Movement in the United States: A Study in American Philanthropy* (New York: MacMillan, 1922); for New York, see Lillian B. Brandt, "Growth and Development of AICP and COS: A Preliminary and Exploratory Review" (paper prepared for the Community Service Society, New York, 1942; and *The Charity Organization Society of the City of New York, 1882–1907: Twenty-fifth Annual Report for the Year Ending September Thirtieth, Nineteen Hundred and Seven* (New York: United Charities Building, 1907).

philanthropist's drawing room, or a legislator's desk in the state capitol.[4] The point is best made through the stories of individual families. Here are excerpts from the lives of three of the poorest families in early-twentieth-century New York City.

Rose Warrington

Rose Warrington was born in Jersey City in 1878. When she was four years old, her parents died, and she went to live with her only relative, a sister in New York City. When Rose was fourteen, her sister also died, and she moved as a servant into the home of an old woman next door. With almost no schooling, illiterate, unable even to sign her name, she remained there until at the age of eighteen she married George Jackson, who worked for the Street Cleaning Department. Together, they had five children, of whom four survived. Suddenly, in 1907, after an illness of only two weeks, George Jackson died of "galloping consumption," leaving only a purse collected by his workmates. Within two years, eager to find a father for her children, Rose married her lodger, Daniel Warrington. Daniel also had been married before. He and his wife had kept a saloon for ten years until his drinking became intolerable and she left him. Now, her former marriage a secret from her neighbors, she lived with another man as his wife. Daniel's drinking cost him work. A talented plumber and, when sober, an excellent, reliable workman, he was fired reluctantly by employers no longer willing to tolerate his periodic sprees.

At first the Warringtons lived with their four children and an orphaned niece who, Rose thought, corrupted her older daughter, Mabel. Daniel was not a devoted stepfather, and neighbors and school officials reported the family for neglect to the Society for the Prevention of Cruelty to Children, which successfully prosecuted it and sent the children from her first marriage to institutions, leaving her with Sadie, John, and her baby, Rose. Whatever his failings as a step-

---

[4] I have written extended stories from the clients' viewpoints in *Poverty and Policy in American History* (New York: Academic Press, 1983), chap. 1; and "The History of an Impudent Poor Woman in New York City from 1918 to 1923," in Peter Mandler, ed., *The Uses of Charity* (Philadelphia: University of Pennsylvania Press, 1991), pp. 227–46.

father, Daniel managed to provide for his family until a prolonged bout of unemployment in 1917. By every indication, too, he was devoted to his wife and children. Nonetheless, depressed about his lack of a job, one morning he went to look for work and never returned.

Unable to support herself, Rose turned to the Charity Organization Society, which took up her case. Not only did it provide funds itself, it persuaded a local Catholic church to help the family. One of its agents tracked down Daniel's relatives, who began to send money anonymously.

When the Charity Organization Society's visitor paid her regular call in December 1918, she found the family had moved. The reason, she discovered, was that Daniel suddenly had returned. Passionately attached to him, Rose had accepted his return without question. Together, the family had moved to a nearby but better apartment, and Daniel had begun to support his family once again. When she found them, the visitor reported Rose as "radiantly happy." Self-sufficient now, no longer in need of charity—indeed, Daniel offered to pay back the Society for the help it had given his family—Rose and Daniel treated the visitor cordially and invited her to call for tea whenever she was in the neighborhood. Daniel said that he had left to teach his wife a lesson: she should appreciate him more and not listen to those— meaning his in-laws—who would interfere. From organized charity's point of view, one problem remained. Despite her denials, the Charity Organization Society suspected Rose and Daniel never had been legally married, and they gave their opinion to the local priest, who visited the couple. Rose was very angry, as she told the visitor when she returned. Rose did not invite the Charity Organization Society to call again.

Mary O'Brien

Mary O'Brien, born in Ireland in 1865, emigrated to New York when she was seventeen. She worked as a waitress for four years and then married Patrick Murphy, a stableman, born five years earlier than Mary. Patrick had arrived in New York in 1883, at the age of twenty-three. By 1895, they had five children. Patrick worked steadily at a stable until 1895, when he was laid off because business was bad. His next job lasted only two months. For a while the family managed to live on the generosity of neighbors until, on the edge of starvation, they applied for charity. A small donation from the Association for Improving the Condition of the Poor tided the family over until Patrick found another job, and the family retained its independence for five years. However, between 1900 and 1910, it asked help from the Charity Organization Society on thirteen different occasions.

A series of work-related accidents coupled with chronic ill health kept Patrick from work and left his family periodically destitute. In August 1900, a horse stepped on his foot; in May 1903, a horse kicked him; in February 1905, while he was shoveling snow for the Metropolitan Street Railway, his feet froze; in August 1907, the heat at the Metropolitan Stables prostrated him. Even when uninjured, he suffered from colds and debilitating rheumatism.

Illness and pregnancy eroded Mary's earning power, too, although she often supported her family. Between 1901 and 1905, she gave birth to three more children, one of whom died. She suffered, too, from jaundice, periodic general ill health, menopause, and recurrent depression and discouragements. She found a variety of menial jobs, all of which paid badly. She washed towels for four cents a dozen; did five people's laundry for seventy-five cents; cleaned part-time in Altman's and elsewhere for about two-to-four dollars a week; served for a time as a housekeeper, taking care of her own and a neighboring tenement for her rent and eight dollars a month in cash; worked at the Charity Organization Society's laundry for eighty cents a day; cleaned hotels and boardinghouses from 7 A.M. to 9 P.M.; and did "day's work," sometimes found by organized charity, which supplied private individuals with cheap, reliable domestic help. The children helped, too, working after school or looking after the baby.

Despite Mary's efforts, the Charity Organization Society remained suspicious of the family. Its representatives could not understand why Patrick did not work. He was, they thought, simply lazy. In 1907, the family's destitution notwithstanding, the Charity Organization Society finally decided to stop all financial aid. Nonetheless, "because of the children," it kept the case open, visiting, advising, and offering help with jobs, medical care, and schools. Its purpose was to goad Patrick back to regular, full-time work. Its visitors knew the price:

151

Mary's exploitation as the family's breadwinner and the destitution of the children.

A few months later, desperate for help, Mary told the Charity Organization visitor the secret of why Patrick did not work. When he was a child, he had burned his left hand. Over time, the muscles had contracted, and the hand was almost useless. He had managed fairly well with his right hand until in recent years rheumatism had weakened it. Patrick said he did not often talk about his hand because he feared it would prevent him from obtaining work.

The Murphys suffered from still another problem. Their daughter Ann was mentally deficient. As she reached adolescence, the Charity Organization visitor began to worry about the consequences of her developing sexuality. The only solution, she felt, was an institution, and she began a long, eventually successful campaign to persuade the Murphys to place her in one. In the course of the procedure, the Charity Organization Society managed to alienate the Murphys by usurping their prerogative to apply to the city's commissioner of public charities themselves. When the Society submitted an application for commitment accompanied by a personal, detailed history of the family, even the city's commissioner of public charities objected.

By the time Ann was institutionalized, the two eldest children, who had reached fourteen, could leave school and take full-time jobs. With Mary working, too, the family could subsist on its own. And so it did, for at least the next decade.

Nellie Park

On the night of March 26, 1904, a great fire burned the Adams Express Company at 59 Broadway. To save his life, Alexander Park, an expressman who worked for American Express, which rented space on the fifth floor (its main building was next door), jumped out a window. Injured from his fall, never able to work again, he received a little help from the St. Vincent de Paul Conference of a local Catholic church and half-pay from American Express. On May 29, 1910, at the age of thirty-four, he died. When Alexander died, both American Express and the Conference at once stopped their payments. For American

Express, it was a matter of policy; the Conference's decision reflected their expectation that a combination of insurance and the wages that Nellie, Alexander's twenty-six-year-old widow, could earn would support the family. Nellie collected $150 from his life insurance policy with the National Express Employees Benevolent Association and $134.30 from his policy with the Prudential Insurance Company. She spent $168 for his funeral.

Nellie tried to manage on her own, working in a laundry, but the work proved too strenuous, and she switched to cleaning offices for six dollars a week. When eye trouble prevented her from working, she pawned her dress to pay for the eyeglasses prescribed by a doctor. Alexander had left Nellie with three young children, ages seven, five, and one; three others had died. At this time a family of four—so students of the cost of living concluded—needed about fifteen dollars or eighteen dollars a week to survive in New York City. Nellie suffered from more than low wages. Alexander's good intentions had left her unusually inexperienced as a housekeeper. Because he had worked nights, he had stayed at home during the day, helping with the housework and marketing, and lifting customary domestic responsibilities from Nellie, whom he had treated "more or less like a child."

Soon, her depleted resources forced Nellie to move to much less expensive rooms, and she depended increasingly on charity, especially the St. Vincent de Paul Society and the Sisters of Mercy, who for a time brought food every day. Unwell, Nellie visited a doctor, who reported she had incipient tuberculosis in her left lung. In these circumstances, the Charity Organization Society, which had been called into the case, advised that she and her children, about whose health authorities worried, go to asylums. A devoted mother, Nellie resisted giving up her children, and authorities, calling her "obstinate" and "ignorant," chastised her for refusing to follow good advice. By April 1911, Nellie capitulated. Threatened with eviction, pressured from all sides, she agreed to go to a sanitarium at Otisville with her boy, Daniel, and to commit her children to a Roman Catholic orphanage. Homesick for her children, Nellie left Otisville in October. She had gained fifteen pounds and felt much better. She tried briefly to manage with all her children but, unable to support them, arranged for the

153

commitment of the two youngest to a home, where they remained. She and Daniel lived briefly with her sister, whose husband, a waiter earning only eight dollars a week, refused to allow them to stay very long. Undoubtedly, he objected both to the expense and to the fact that his wife and child along with Rose and Daniel all shared one bed.

Nellie went back to laundry work, against all medical advice, and managed without help for four years. She and Daniel lived in a succession of furnished rooms until they found a small, badly ventilated three-room apartment. Daniel was supposed to attend a day camp for youngsters at risk of tuberculosis. Sometimes he went; sometimes he took the carfare and played on the streets. All the authorities concerned with the case considered him not only wild but stupid. They referred, disparagingly, to his "mental condition." They wanted him put in an institution, but Nellie objected.

Whatever authorities thought about his "mental condition," Daniel was a leader among his peers. Youngsters on the street thronged around him to hear his stories. Clever and resourceful, he made more money than any of the other young boys who hung around a local theater selling candy and peanuts. On one election day, he earned fifty cents peddling apples. He also found marginally licit ways of scavenging coal for his mother.

Indeed, Daniel was devoted to his mother, who, in turn, doted on him, despite their frequent quarrels. He sold papers to help her and earned bits of money with which to take her to the movies.

For a variety of reasons, Daniel had never attended school. When he began, his teachers' assessments proved surprising. Daniel, they felt, was intelligent. He worked industriously and performed well. His teachers liked him very much. His health improved, too. He did not, after all, have tuberculosis. Nellie seemed to be managing competently; her apartment always was clean and her clothes attractive. Even though her wages remained wretched, she worked steadily. Still, neither Nellie's independence nor Daniel's improved health, success in school, and devotion to his mother altered the Charity Organization Society's plan for the Park family. It wanted to send Nellie to a sanitarium and Daniel to an institution. When Nellie continued to resist, the Charity Organization Society enlisted a male visitor from the Catholic Big Brothers, a Mr. Gleason. Even he could not convince her.

Determined to prevail, Mr. Gleason and the Charity Organization Society looked for further ammunition. When a doctor diagnosed Nellie as tubercular, the Charity Organization Society moved quickly to enlist the help of the Society for the Prevention of Cruelty to Children (SPCC), which prosecuted the case. As part of the proceedings Nellie underwent still another and more careful examination, which showed she was not tubercular. Nellie "never has had a positive sputum," reported the clinic. The SPCC's officer worried that this finding might undercut the case, but he felt strongly that Nellie was "a menace and . . . unable to care for Daniel as he should be cared for." The court agreed and committed him to the Mission of the Immaculate Virgin.

When Nellie met the Charity Organization Society's visitor a month later, she was indignant. The judge had told her that the Society had "done the whole business," and the SPCC said the same thing. Nellie wanted nothing more to do with organized charity. Nellie's information was right, as the Society's distorted letter to the SPCC describing the history of her case revealed.

Still, eventually she made her peace with both Daniel's incarceration and the Charity Organization Society. When the visitor met her on the street sometime later, she reported she was managing financially by doing odd bits of sewing and caring for neighborhood women when they gave birth. She appeared, said the visitor, "well satisfied to have Daniel away and seemed rather inclined to follow the suggestion of visitor to take this opportunity to go away and get herself in good condition and perhaps by the time Daniel has graduated from the school and is able to work, that she will be strong and able to care for her family."

Surviving Poverty: Themes

These stories are excerpts from detailed case histories of families in the files of New York City's Charity Organization Society from the late-nineteenth and early-twentieth century. Wealthy, philanthropic New Yorkers created the Charity Organization Society (COS) in 1882 to eliminate fraud and reduce dependency. The COS investigated applicants to other relief societies and offered support and advice through friendly visiting. Modeled on the Charity Organization Society in Britain, it was, as chapter 1 noted, one of many such agencies founded throughout the country in the same period. By the twentieth century, contrary to its original model, it also gave relief. The COS worked closely with the city's largest relief organization, the Association for Improving the Condition of the Poor (AICP), founded by Robert Hartley in 1843. To coordinate their efforts, in the mid-1890s, the AICP and COS established a Joint Application Bureau, which received requests for help and parceled them out to the appropriate society. In 1939, the two organizations joined to form the Community Service Society.

The COS divided New York City into districts, each with its own office headed by a district secretary and staffed by paid visitors, or agents. Visitors had authority to offer emergency assistance, but the district committee made decisions about long-term care. Committees, comprising representatives of the principal professions and religious denominations, generally met weekly. The COS central office maintained a registry of cases and performed other functions, including organizing specialized committees to consider citywide problems. It also sponsored social research and the first social work training in the city.

The Society for the Prevention of Cruelty to Children was the other great agency that looms large in these stories. Organized first in 1876 in New York City, it investigated complaints of child neglect and abuse. Its quasi-police powers permitted the SPCC to require the police to investigate complaints, charge parents in court, and request the commitment of children to institutions. It also served a quasi-penal function, incarcerating children held for trial, removed temporarily from their homes, or awaiting institutional placement. Poor people, who feared it, gave the SPCC its popular name, "the Cruelty."[5]

In 1875, New York City stopped giving public outdoor relief to poor

---

[5] There is useful information on the SPCC in George K. Behlmer, *Child Abuse and Moral Reform in England, 1870–1908* (Stanford, Calif.: Stanford University Press, 1982); Catherine J. Ross, "Society's Children: The Care of Indigent Youngsters in New York City, 1875–1903" (Ph.D. dissertation, Yale University, 1977); and Linda Gordon, *Heroes of Their Own Lives: The Politics and History of Family Violence, Boston, 1880–1960* (New York: Viking, 1988).

people. It still assisted the needy blind and, until prevented in the 1890s by a successful campaign spearheaded by the COS, distributed free coal. Nonetheless, the city still contributed large sums to help dependent people. Most of these were spent through institutions. The city operated an almshouse, workhouse, municipal lodging house, and various hospitals. The city's courts assisted families by prosecuting husbands for desertion and nonsupport and by placing children in institutions. Both the city and state paid the fees of children in private orphanages, including ones run by religious denominations. In 1893, one of every thirty-five children in New York City lived in an orphange supported by public funds.[6] "As early as 1890, 57% of all public expenditures on aid to the poor in New York City went to support services provided through nonprofit organizations," points out Lester Salamon.[7] Public funds also sustained voluntary hospitals.

Catholic institutions, such as the enormous Catholic Protectory, were the primary beneficiaries of public funding. Through the local chapters of the St. Vincent de Paul Society, Catholics also assisted great numbers of their poor. The United Hebrew Charities, the city's other major relief agency, assisted poor Jews; in 1900 alone, it investigated 31,088 applications for relief, and its employment bureau placed 6,594 persons in work.[8]

Many other agencies and charities populated the city with a complex network not described usefully as either public or private. Every year, the Charity Organization Society listed them in its *New York Charities Directory*, which in 1900 consisted of about 620 pages, excluding the index and advertisements, that mapped a vast, intricate, complicated terrain to be negotiated by those in need of help.[9]

[6] Ross, "Society's Children," p. 154; *Humanizing the Greater City's Charity: The Work of the Department of Public Charities of the City of New York* (Public Welfare Committee, 50 East Forty-Second Street, New York, 1917); *New York Charities Directory* (Charity Organization Society of the City of New York, 1900).

[7] Lester M. Salamon, "The Nonprofit Sector and Government: The American Experience in Theory and Practice," in Helmut K. Anheier and Wolfgang Seibel, eds., *The Third Sector: Comparative Studies of Nonprofit Organizations* (Berlin: Walter de Gruyter, 1990), p. 226.

[8] *New York Charities Directory*, p. 97.

[9] John Mohr, "Community, Bureaucracy, and Social Relief: An Institutional Analysis of Organizational Forms in New York City, 1888–1917" (Ph.D. dissertation, Yale University, 1992).

In no time period in the city's history was that terrain's negotiation as difficult, for these years spanned a transformation of New York City's demography, economy, and society. Fueled by new immigrants from eastern and southern Europe, the city's population exploded from 2,300,000 in 1890 to 4,766,000 only twenty years later. Among these, Italians, Jews, Rumanians, Syrians, and others new in large numbers to America remade the population's composition. Throughout these years, nearly two of every three New York City residents were immigrants or their children. By 1930, 440,000 Italian immigrants lived in New York City. All but 82,000 had arrived after 1901; the growth trajectory of the city's 238,000 Polish and 442,000 Russian immigrants had followed the same pattern.

At the same time, industrialization altered the city's economy. New York never became the site of massive manufacturing. Instead, small firms clustered especially in the clothing, printing and publishing, and luxury trades dotted the city with their shops, factories, and sweatshops. Between 1880 and 1910, workers in these industries accounted for 70 percent of the increase in the city's industrial wage earners. Increasingly, too, the city's economy reflected the emergence of large national corporations, which, from their base in Manhattan, coordinated vast operations throughout the country. As always, too, the city remained a center of finance and shipping. Between 1880 and 1910, the number of national manufacturing firms with assets of $1 million or more located in New York City increased more than ten times, from 32 to 330.[10]

Although immigrants often clustered together in distinct sections of the city, New York's neighborhoods, apart from the Lower East Side, remained remarkably diverse. Indeed, social diversity underlay the Charity Organization Society's strategy, which assumed the presence in each of its districts of enough educated and well-off persons, knowl-

[10] Figures and information on New York's development come from David C. Hammack, *Power and Society: Greater New York at the Turn of the Century* (New York: Russell Sage Foundation, 1982), chaps. 2 and 3; Ira Rosenwaike, *Population History of New York City* (Syracuse, N.Y.: Syracuse University Press, 1972), chaps. 4 and 5 and apps. A–C; Emanuel Tobier, "Manhatten's Business District in the Industrial Age," in John Hull Mollenkopf, ed., *Power, Culture, and Place: Essays on New York City* (New York: Russell Sage Foundation, 1988), pp. 77–105.

edgeable about local conditions, to serve on its committees and provide a pool of volunteer friendly visitors. By late in the nineteenth century, only for the lower portion of Manhattan did this assumption prove untenable.

As a microcosm of working class New York, consider the demography of one of the tenements that housed Rose Warrington and her family, whose story I sketched earlier. Among the fourteen families crowded into the tenement on Second Avenue just above 125th Street were an Austrian railroad guard, a German widow, an Austrian waiter, an Italian driver, a Hungarian printer, a Russian railway conductor, an Austrian woman who ran a fruit store, an American driver for an express company, a Finnish carpenter, a Finnish stonecutter, an Italian tailor, and an American laborer on the subway. This ethnic diversity and mix of nonindustrial working-class occupations reflected the composition of the neighborhood, with the notable exception of the block of East 127th Street east of Third Avenue, where nearly all the residents were black.[11]

The case histories of the COS show how families with incomes far below the poverty lines drawn by contemporary researchers managed to survive. They transform these people from one-dimensional stereotypes into individuals, struggling, loving, coping, above all, being human. Although many common themes run throughout these stories, no one case is typical. Their message, rather, is the individuality, resourcefulness, and resilience of ordinary people. Like the best ethnographies of the present, they reveal a *variety* that underscores a crucial lesson for policy. Images of very poor people implicit in public policy and social science too often sketch bleak portraits of populations uniformly disorganized, apathetic, incompetent, and amoral. As a consequence, policy makers and researchers miss the variegated patterns of relationships and activities within even the most disadvantaged neighborhoods, the individuality of persons, and the strategies they deploy to survive their poverty.

Set within a dynamic, diverse, changing city, Rose Warrington's story and those of the other families assisted by the Charity Organiza-

---

[11] New York State Census, 1915, Office of the New York County Clerk, 60 Chambers St., room 141b.

tion Society illustrate themes related to four major topics: routes into and out of dependence; family and gender; housing, space, and mobility; and the social construction of moral worth and the social relations of charity.

Consider first the origins of dependence. Families found themselves dependent because of irregular work, accidents, widowhood, illness, and lack of child care. Most cases, in fact, reflected some combination of these factors; as a result, dependence usually was overdetermined. With men, the irregularity of work created more of a problem than their low wages did. Charity officials thought any steadily employed man, unless handicapped by an exceptionally large number of children, able to support his family. Most working-class men, however, could not save enough to survive their recurrent bouts of unemployment. Women, also subject to seasonal unemployment, earned a fraction of men's wages. Alone, even a steadily employed widow rarely could support herself and more than one child. For this reason, organized charity often supplemented widows' wages. Indeed, supplementing wages, at least for widows, appeared to arouse less controversy at the time than do similar policies today.

Patrick Murphy's history of accidents, described earlier, was by no means unusual. America experienced the highest rate of workplace accidents in the industrialized world.[12] Accidents were one reason why sickness was so important a cause of destitution; beyond accidents, a host of illnesses plagued poor people. In these years, the worst, of course, was tuberculosis. In 1914 and 1915, New York City's register of tuberculosis patients numbered 35,000, with 22,000 new cases added each year. Of these, 8,918 died. Their care cost public and private sources $687,342.00.[13] Sickness, in fact, forms a major thread running throughout nearly every family's story. In almost none of them could the family afford to pay for its own medical care. For this reason, free medical care formed a principal component in the relief of

[12] James Weinstein, "Big Business and the Origins of Workmen's Compensation," *Labor History* 8:2 (spring 1967): 157; Carl Gersuny, *Work Hazards and Industrial Conflict* (Hanover, N.H.: University Press of New England, 1981), pp. 20, 28.

[13] [Miss Hurlbutt] Association of Tuberculosis Clinics of New York City, "Study of Homes," August 18, 1916, typescript, "Studies—Joint Committtee on Homes" folder, box 162, Community Service Society collection, Rare Book and Manuscript Room, Butler Library, Columbia University.

dependence, and the authority of professional medicine, delivered through dispensaries, clinics, and hospitals, often shaped the day-to-day experience of the poor.[14]

Poor people moved in and out of dependence. Could we reconstruct them systematically, patterns would look much like those uncovered by the Michigan Income Panel Dynamics Study in recent years, only the proportions would be much higher. Many families experienced recurrent spells of dependence; some stayed in them for a very long time. Almost all working-class families, however, lived, as one writer put it, on the verge of dependence.[15] I use *dependence* rather than *poverty* because most of these families, even when they managed on their own, were poor by any reasonable standards. Indeed, poverty was the normal state for close to half the city's population. Of these, a floating subset could not survive without outside help.

For these families, help did not come often from the city's political machines. Despite the image of benevolence cultivated by machine politicians themselves and perpetuated by historians, none of these families reported gifts of cash, food, clothing, housing, or medical assistance from political sources. In a very few instances, men received jobs on public works, especially building the subways, through political connections. My suspicion—and more research on this topic is needed—is that historians have exaggerated greatly the amount of concrete assistance provided by political machines. For the most part, machines reached the working class by controlling access to public jobs. In this, they proved of more use to the working than the dependent poor, the most needy New Yorkers, who were by and large women, children, or partially disabled men unable to perform strenuous physical labor.[16] Perhaps the dependent poor were not of much

[14] David Rosner, *A Once Charitable Enterprise: Hospitals and Health Care in Brooklyn and New York, 1885–1915* (New York: Cambridge University Press, 1982); Charles Rosenberg, "Social Class and Medical Care in the United States: The Rise and Fall of the Dispensary," in Judith Walzer Leavitt and Ronald L. Numbers, eds., *Sickness and Health in America: Readings in the History of Medicine and Public Health* (Madison: University of Wisconsin Press, 1978), pp. 151–71.

[15] Lillian Brandt, "On the Verge of Dependence," *Charities and Commons* 15 (1905–6): 462–68.

[16] On political machines, see Steven P. Erie, *Rainbow's End: Irish Americans and the Dilemmas of Urban Machine Politics, 1840–1985* (Berkeley and Los Angeles: University of California Press, 1988).

interest to local politicians on account of their age, gender, or citizen-ship, or because they voted only infrequently.

Families emerged from dependence because men found jobs, women remarried, governments granted pensions, or children went to work. Two of these routes require some comment. Early in the century, some women remained eligible for Civil War pensions, extended to surviving family members of Northern veterans late in the nine-teenth century. After 1916, a small but significant number of widows received the state's new mothers' pensions. Although small, when combined with wages from a job such as cleaning offices (an emerging form of employment that fit mothers' schedules), mothers' pensions enabled women with children to survive. Much more common, how-ever, was the labor of children. Children left school at fourteen—if they were reluctant, the COS usually managed to persuade them oth-erwise—and found jobs. Most of these paid badly, to start perhaps four dollars a week for a messenger or three or four dollars a week for a sweatshop worker. Still, together with their mothers' wages, chil-dren's earnings provided enough to assure the independence of their families. With remarkable willingness, most youngsters accepted their role, for which, of course, they paid a heavy price in forgone prospects for mobility. Indeed, many families escaped dependence on the backs of their children.[17]

Survival strategies of poor people in America's cities remained, it now appears, more or less similar until after World War II, as the work of Kathryn Neckerman, among others, shows. Among these strategies, reliance on children's wages was nearly universal. Only in the 1950s, according to Mark Stern's analysis of census data, did this reliance on children's wages start to decline. In the long run, chil-dren's wages have not been replaced by high incomes for male house-holders, which, after growing for a couple of decades after World War II, have declined during the last twenty years. Rather, the wages of married women, who have entered the wage workforce in unprece-

[17] Michael B. Katz, *In the Shadow of the Poorhouse: A Social History of Welfare in America* (New York: Basic Books, 1986), p. 201; Susan Tiffin, *In Whose Best Interest? Child Welfare Reform in the Progressive Era* (Westport, Conn.: Greenwood Press, 1982), pp. 121–30, 232–37; Roy Lubove, *The Struggle for Social Security, 1900–1935* (Cambridge: Harvard University Press, 1968), pp. 91–112.

dented numbers during the last few decades, have substituted for those of children.[18]

Education as a source of social mobility played almost no role in these stories about New York's poorest families. Only two or three children from the families in these case histories appear to have entered the expanding world of white-collar work. Undoubtedly, rudimentary literacy skills learned in school proved essential for a variety of jobs and for navigating the city's network of public and private institutions and agencies. However, once these children reached working age, for them and their families school was an obstacle to employment, not an avenue of opportunity.

For the most part, New York's poor lived in nuclear families with few kin relations other than parents and children. Some, especially widows, took in boarders, a practice organized charity viewed with ambivalence. Boarders meant extra income, which could boost a family over the line to independence. Nonetheless, charity officials and reformers thought families and boarders crammed together in congested rooms posed a menace to health and morals. In any event, few stayed very long, and actual household composition frequently shifted.

The behavior of clients' relatives, where it can be traced, usually reflected ambivalence. Certainly, they believed in their moral obligation to assist their needy kin. None of them whose remarks I have read asserted that relatives could lay no claims on each other, but they, too, usually were either poor or on the verge of dependence, afraid that a modicum of help might be misconstrued as the down payment on regular assistance, fearful of entrapment by an obligation with no clear end. In these circumstances, relatives followed various courses: material assistance, outright refusal, anonymous donations, and the invention of reasons why their kin did not merit their assistance. In practice, they vacillated between these courses, their guilt and fear evident in their inconsistency.

Wives, too, often revealed ambivalence about their spouses. Many, wanting support from reluctant or deserting husbands, unhesitatingly

[18] Neckerman, "The Emergence of Underclass Family Patterns, 1900–1940"; and Stern, "Poverty and Family Composition since 1940."

charged them in Magistrates', later Domestic Relations, Court.[19] Others vacillated. However, like Rose Warrington, all the ones in these stories quickly took back their spouses from sprees, flings, or jail. Whether it was a mark of their affection or a sign of their need for a man's wage often remains unclear, but whatever their motive, separation clearly was as likely a temporary as a permanent state.

The most intense bonds united mothers and their children, especially sons.[20] The men in these stories often were indifferent husbands, but their sons rarely neglected their mothers. Like Daniel Park, they worked hard to support and protect them, turning over to them with almost no recorded complaints nearly all their wages. Most mothers, in turn, fought fiercely to preserve their families intact. Although many, in the end, found themselves forced by circumstances to commit children to an institution, most did so with the greatest reluctance. Against the advice of organized charity, they resisted, preferring starvation to separation. Whether or not to break up a family persisted, in fact, as one of the most difficult and often debated questions among charity workers and COS district committees.

Institutions mediated family relations. Whatever an institution's official goals, poor people themselves turned it partly to their own purposes. Courts became arenas for the resolution of family conflicts, orphanages temporary shelters for children during times of family crisis, and hospitals sources of nourishment and child care.[21] Indeed, most of the families in the case histories discriminated among the city's hospitals, resisting some strongly, seeking admittance to others.

No one generalization describes the role of institutions and social agencies in the lives of these families. At times, they proved callous,

[19] New York City established a separate Domestic Relations Court in 1910. Magistrates also heard complaints involving nonsupport and desertion. Raymond Moley, *Tribunes of the People: The Past and Future of the New York Magistrates' Courts* (New Haven: Yale University Press, 1932), p. 29.

[20] In this sense, relations between mothers and sons echo those described by D. H. Lawrence in *Sons and Lovers* (New York: Boni and Liveright, 1989).

[21] For examples of the transformation of institutional purposes by inmates and their families, see Barbara M. Brenzel, *Daughters of the State: A Social Portrait of the First Reform School for Girls in North America, 1846–1905* (Cambridge: MIT Press, 1983); and Allen Steinberg, *The Transformation of Criminal Justice: Philadelphia, 1800–1880* (Chapel Hill: University of North Carolina Press, 1989).

condescending, even indifferent. Yet institutions could prove helpful, enabling families to survive crises, offering decent, thoughtful care, helping to resolve disputes. Looked at one way, institutions reinforced existing social relations, with education, for example, through the limited schooling offered poor children; policed poor people, as when their agents broke up families; and helped keep wages low by, for example, forcing poor women to work for a pittance in their laundries, which took in the washing of the well-to-do. Institutions and agencies often concentrated more on improving poor people, changing values and behavior, than on dealing with the material sources of their problems. Nonetheless, institutions and social agencies not only provided essential services; many individuals employed in them cared deeply about the families with whom they worked and subordinated social ideology to practical assistance; and institutions often remained malleable, partially reshaped to serve the needs of their clients. Inconsistent institutional and agency actions resulted from their limited resources and heavy burden, the intrusion of state and local politics, the handicap of rigid ideology, and the multiple, often conflicting purposes they served, as with welfare and education, described in previous chapters.

Shelter, as well as food, medicine, and clothing, preoccupied New York's poor. Many of their histories read as a long, unsatisfactory search for decent, cheap housing (a not unfamiliar story throughout the history of New York City). They moved often but usually not very far. Evicted because they failed to pay their rent, they moved next door, down the block, around the corner, rarely out of the neighborhood. Their carefully constructed networks of personal assistance, friendship, and credit bound them within narrow spheres, and the expense of carfare meant they could not afford to live far from where they worked.[22]

Networks constituted the primary "social capital" that facilitated

[22] The residential patterns in these cases are similar to those described by Gareth Stedman Jones in *Outcast London* (London: Oxford University Press, 1971). On housing in New York in this period see *The Progressives and the Slums: Tenement House Reform in New York City, 1890–1917* (Pittsburgh: University of Pittsburgh Press, 1962); and Donna R. Gabaccia, *From Sicily to Elizabeth Street: Housing and Social Change among Italian Immigrants, 1880–1930* (Albany: State University of New York Press, 1984).

poor people's survival. With no tangible and little "human" capital in the form of education or vocational skills, they depended on the relations built up with friends, relatives, merchants, social agencies, and landlords. These relations cut two ways, serving as capital on which they could draw in their daily struggles for food, fuel, and shelter but also trapping them, circumscribing their sense of possibilities as well as limiting their opportunities. It would be instructive to learn if the networks that constitute social capital play a similar part in both ameliorating and reinforcing concentrated poverty in today's inner cities.[23]

Landlords were major players in the stories of New York's poor. A good landlord not only kept his buildings well repaired, he or she also allowed tenants to run up a bill for back rent. Landlords faced a dilemma: if they ejected tenants when they failed to pay, they were unlikely ever to collect any part of the rent. Nor was it likely that they would fill their rooms with anyone significantly more affluent. Still, if they were too lenient, if they never took action, they could find themselves permanently with no income from their property. The resolution of this dilemma meant calibrating the relation between potential loss and income with care. Individual landlords differed in the way they reached their decisions, as reflected in the amount of time they allowed to pass before they went to the court for an order to evict. But nearly all of them, by permitting some leeway, served de facto as important creditors of the poor.

Within nearly every tenement—and, remember, New York was a city of tenements—landlords hired a housekeeper or janitress. These women lived rent free in exchange for cleaning the building, showing apartments to prospective tenants, supervising their conduct, and occasionally collecting rent. Their social origins lay in the same class as the tenants themselves. Sometimes they even were clients of organized charity. Indeed, a poor widow performed a difficult calculus in deciding whether to accept a post as housekeeper. True, it meant free rent, but how would she buy food? If her children did not work, she

[23] Robert D. Putnam, *Making Democracy Work: Civic Traditions in Modern Italy* (Princeton: Princeton University Press, 1993); Jones, *Outcast London*.

would probably lack cash, because most landlords forbade their housekeepers from working off the premises. Housekeepers, moreover, lived with a potentially draining tension. They were at once agents of landlords, the eyes and ears of organized charity, and members of a network of informants about families strung out across the city. Yet, given the similarity in class background, they often empathized with and liked their tenants. Caught between conflicting pulls, housekeepers composed a vast, shifting, marginal stratum within the city's social structure.[24]

Because New York was a city of tenements, housekeepers almost certainly were more prominent than in cities such as Philadelphia and Buffalo, where families much more often lived in small houses than in tenements. Whether another group in these cities played a role parallel to New York City's housekeepers is not known. As indigenous agents of the respectable classes reporting on the behavior of neighbors and helping to enforce order, New York City's housekeepers proved so useful that it is reasonable to imagine another set of individuals doing the same work in different settings. Indeed, it is intriguing to ask who, if anyone, acts in this capacity in contemporary inner cities. Perhaps one consequence of urban ecological and demographic change, and of the concentration and isolation of the inner-city poor, has been the disappearance of semi-institutionalized, indigenous agents of information and control. The task now falls to agents of the state—policemen, social workers, teachers—whose association with the people they serve is not nearly so intimate as the housekeepers' of late-nineteenth- and early-twentieth-century New York City.

Housekeepers' advice contributed to the evaluation of applicants by organized charity. The questions were, Is the applicant worthy? Does the family deserve charity? Drawing the line between the worthy and unworthy poor has remained an insoluble problem. No society has ever controlled enough resources to meet everyone's needs. The difficulty is defining the boundary, which must always be a social con-

---

[24] There is no literature on housekeepers or janitors. I have arrived at these conclusions from reading the case records.

struct, a reflection of judgment and values rather than of science and objective evidence.[25] As in contemporary debates over welfare or the "underclass," this is no less true today than it was in the past.

To organized charity, personal worth rested on behavior, attitude, and class. The three criteria for judging behavior involved sex, alcohol, and truthfulness. Of these, sexual misconduct was the most serious and lying the least. Charity workers knew that everyone lied a little bit. The problem was to prevent it from becoming excessive. The situation has parallels today. Kathryn Edin and Christopher Jencks discovered that women cannot survive solely on AFDC benefits. All of the women Edin interviewed supplement their AFDC in some way, all, of course, illegally. As a result, they are forced to lie to their caseworkers, who know what is happening but, in most instances, choose not to investigate or enforce the rules literally. This situation gives caseworkers enormous, arbitrary power over the lives of their clients, as it did early in the century as well.[26]

Charity workers also accepted, if unwillingly, that most people drank a little. Only when drinking translated into incapacity for work, domestic violence, or an excessive financial drain did COS workers assert their authority. Sexuality was another matter. COS officials defined not just prostitution but any sex outside marriage as illicit, and they often pried relentlessly into the behavior of adolescents and young widows. Although sexual standards have relaxed during the last century, whether welfare clients are seen by officials and the public as possessing the same sexual rights as other citizens remains an open question.

Readiness to work, willingness to take advice, and gratitude were the three most desirable attitudes. The Charity Organization Society often cut off help to clients because they thought they were lazy or because they refused to take advice. Contemporary proposals for "workfare" try, with limited success, to accomplish the same ends. At

[25] I have dealt with this problem at length in *The Undeserving Poor: From the War on Poverty to the War on Welfare* (New York: Pantheon, 1990).

[26] Kathryn Edin and Christopher Jencks, "Reforming Welfare," in Christopher Jencks, ed., *Rethinking Social Policy: Race, Poverty, and the Underclass* (Cambridge: Harvard University Press, 1992), pp. 204–36.

the same time, they wanted their help accepted with gratitude, for, as a gift, charity always has been partly about deference and reciprocity. Organized charity expected its clients to express their gratitude, and visitors almost always noted when they did.[27] More than any other response, a sense of entitlement, the opposite of gratitude, annoyed charity visitors. (Observe the persistence today of this connection among deference, gratitude, and charity in many solicitations that personalize recipients. As another example, the public image of the homeless became increasingly unfavorable as they exchanged their pathetic, passive self-presentation for a more assertive, decidedly undeferential stance.) Nonetheless, the presence of children who were both blameless and vulnerable frequently checked the Charity Organization Society's desire to stop its help, even when it assessed a family as undeserving. As in the story of the Murphys, which I told earlier, the phrase "because of the children" explained the COS's continued aid to a family about whose character it retained grave doubts. As for class, a few clients had experienced downward mobility. Through bad luck or bad management they had lost wealth and position. Whatever the reason for their fall, their evident gentility always earned them favorable consideration by the Charity Organization Society, despite behavior that would have assigned a client of humble origins to classification as a member of the undeserving poor. Still, assignment to categories of worth remained provisional, and assessments of individual clients frequently reversed during the years they remained under the care and supervision of organized charity.

Two examples illustrate how and why organized charity changed its opinion of families and how the relations between its officials and their clients played themselves out in decisions about whether to give or withhold aid. The stories of Matilda Gehrig and the Brighams show both this protean quality of evaluation and the social relations of charity that they exemplify.

The Charity Organization Society first helped Matilda Gehrig, a worthy Austrian widow with small children, in 1893. By sewing fringe at home, Matilda earned about four dollars a week. Her parents,

---

[27] On the relation between charity and gratitude, see Jones, *Outcast London*, p. 253.

themselves poor and dependent on her brother, lived in another apartment in the same building. With a little charity and some decent medical care—for Matilda was in the early stages of tuberculosis—she stabilized her income enough to convince the Charity Organization Society, though not others who knew her, that she could manage on her own.

Within a few years, she married Cesar Romero, a gas fitter born in Cuba. Then, in 1892, again a widow, Matilda asked for help once more. By all accounts, Matilda was a meticulous housekeeper and excellent parent, and no one could fault her as lazy or question her morals. Still, her health limited Matilda's options by preventing her from taking heavy tasks or working in a laundry. How could she support herself until her children were old enough to work? Although the COS had no very good plan, Matilda did. Send her and the children to the country, she urged, where they could rent a whole house for the price of a Manhattan tenement, grow some of their food, and find an occasional day's work.

The COS accepted Matilda's plan and set her up in Sussex, New Jersey, where she went to work at once on her vegetable and flower garden. She also had another idea: if the COS would send children to board with her, the fees for their care would allow her to be independent of charity. Matilda seemed an excellent candidate to be a foster parent, and the COS began to send her boarders. Her long, remarkable letters to the district office on the progress of her domestic affairs and the condition of her boarders revealed Matilda as a devoted and skilled foster parent. Under her care, the children sent from New York City thrived happily.

One day Matilda's oldest daughter, Louise, working as a maid in a convalescent home, blurted out that her mother had hoarded five hundred dollars of insurance money in a bank. Louise often exaggerated, and her employer did not believe her assertion. Nonetheless, she reported it to the COS. Armed with a potential revelation of such magnitude, the district secretary herself traveled to Sussex to interrogate Matilda. Matilda broke down. Louise had invented the story about the insurance money; the little she had received all had been spent years ago. But Matilda was not a widow. Her second husband was alive.

Romero was deranged. He had abused Matilda and threatened to kill her if she ever left him. Unable to find work in New York as a gas fitter, he had returned with Matilda and the children to Cuba, where he had family. Matilda left him there and returned to New York. When she heard that he had returned, she asked the COS to move her to the country. She had even tried to live with him for two weeks in Sussex, but he was so crazy and abusive she threw him out.

Matilda had feared to tell the COS. If they knew she was not a widow, she thought, they might stop helping her. But her lie lay heavily on her conscience, and she was relieved to unburden herself. Later, she wrote the district secretary a long letter of explanation and apology, begging for understanding and mercy. The COS checked Matilda's story with her husband's best friend, who confirmed it. Romero was a wreck, drifting from one hostel to another, unable to work. Matilda, better off without him, was, for all practical purposes, a widow.

The COS attitude toward Matilda altered perceptibly after they learned her whole story. For a while, it continued to send her cash, clothes, and a few boarders, though not as many as she wanted. With the flimsiest of reasons, it decided that Matilda should be able to support herself. With no evidence that she treated the children it sent her with anything other than intelligent, loving care, it ended not only her irregular allowance but her boarders. Matilda pleaded with the district secretary to resume sending children. Without them, she pointed out, her small income could not support her family throughout the winter. The COS remained unmoved; Matilda had joined the ranks of the undeserving poor.

Unlike their initial opinion of Matilda Gehrig Romero, the COS always classified the Brighams as unworthy. Their contact with this native-born family of New Yorkers began in 1891. At the time, the elder Brighams already were in their sixties. They lived with a granddaughter; their married son with his large family was in the same building. John Brigham, the father, did not seem very bright. He earned a little money stringing tags for ten cents a thousand. His married son was unemployed. Jennie Brigham, John's wife, clearly did not tell the truth; the story of her life varied every time she repeated it. The family, in fact, appeared to be professional beggars who exploited their granddaughter until she died late in 1891. The COS wanted nothing to do with the family, but again and again, until the second decade of the twentieth century, it could not escape involvement. The reason usually was a request from someone to whom the Brighams had turned for charity, for the Brigham family appeared masters of New York's vast network of potential assistance. During these years John Brigham died, and Jennie's daughter-in-law sent her husband to prison for nonsupport and then left him. None of this changed the COS evaluation. The Brighams, worthless beggars, could support themselves. On June 12, 1911, a COS investigator concluded, "Family consists of woman and son, former aged, latter indolent, irresponsible and both persistent beggars."

Almost one year later, on May 9, 1912, a visitor, looking up another case in the house, stumbled across Jennie Brigham

living on the second floor rear in extreme old age and utter helplessness without care of any kind, without food, covered with vermin and suffering from sores all over her body. The bedding was nothing but rags, strips, and tufts of cotton. One could not even handle them, without its falling into more pieces. The place including the bed and the person was extremely filthy. The cuspidor stood on the stove filled with sputum and tobacco juice, matches etc. The only other occupant at the time of visit, was a cat, whom the old lady said was her only friend; that she had kept her warm. Visitor went out and bought a cotton blanket (49 cents) a pillow slip (8 cents) and a pint of milk (5 cents). Returned and fed her from a spoon about a cupful of the milk slightly heated. Visitor lifted the old lady out of her bed; rearranged the material and covered it with half the blanket. Laid the old woman in it and covered her with the other half; then added a few of the dirty rags to give sufficient warmth. . . . Visitor then returned to D[istrict] O[ffice]. Reported the case at once and D[istrict] S[ecretary] notified the Police Department and was told that the case would be removed to a hosp. at once. . . . May 16, 1912, Telephoned the Harlem Hosp. Learned that Mrs. B. died May 15 at 2:15 P.M.

Index

government, 44–45; state-level administration of, 50–51; used in politics, 29–31.
See also social welfare
welfare capitalism: emergence, growth,
and effectiveness of, 47–48; programs
of, 29
welfare departments: municipal, 46; state-
level, 44, 50
welfare reform: perceived effects of, 19–
20; problems of real, 21
White House Conference on Children
(1909), 43

Wilentz, Sean, 106n.9
Williams, Patricia, 86
Wilson, James Q., 64
Wilson, William Julius, 75–76, 81
Witte, Edwin, 54
Wolfe, Alan, 25
working class, 106
workmen's compensation, 48
Works Progress Administration (WPA),
53–54

Yancey, William L., 70n.15